STICK IT TO YOUR CHOPS

Exercises to propel your drumming technique above and beyond

Kirby Jacobsen

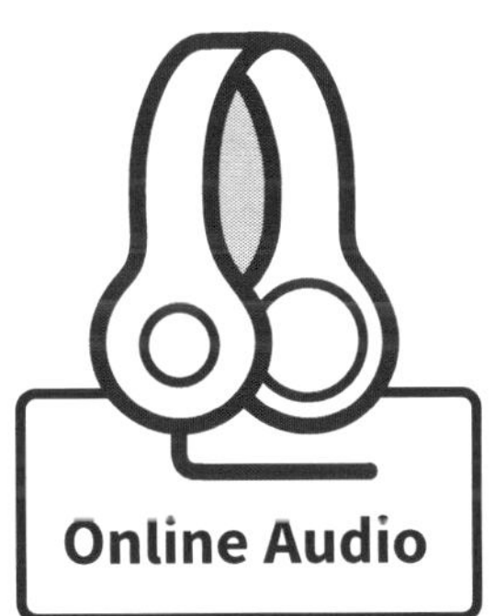

To access the online audio go to:
WWW.MELBAY.COM/31162MEB

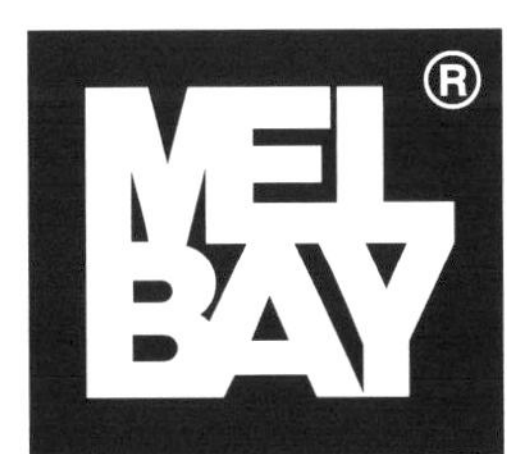

WWW.MELBAY.COM

Contents

Audio Track List

Introduction

The purpose of this book is to advance your technical skills by focusing on three key components: consistency and evenness of strokes, dynamic control and dexterity. This book is not intended to be THE source for developing technique, but more, as a fresh and engaging way of improving your technique. These exercises are challenging, effective and fun to play.

The book consists of three main sections: **Warm-Ups**, **Expanding Accents and Rhythms with Rudiments** and **Combinations**. The **Warm-Ups** section contains exercises to play at the start of practice. **Expanding Accents and Rhythms with Rudiments** employs four common rudiments with accents that are placed further and further apart, as well as groupings that lengthen, in a series of exercises. The **Combinations** section contains every L-R sticking combination in groups of three, four, five, six, seven and eight. In addition, each group has its own RHYTHM CHART which provides an instantly accessible smorgasbord of additional rhythms to apply to the sticking patterns.

All exercises in this book are written with both a right-hand and left-hand lead.

It is important to remember that improving technical skills should serve to enhance your musicianship; a vehicle through which you may ultimately execute ideas with greater ease, smoothness and consistency.

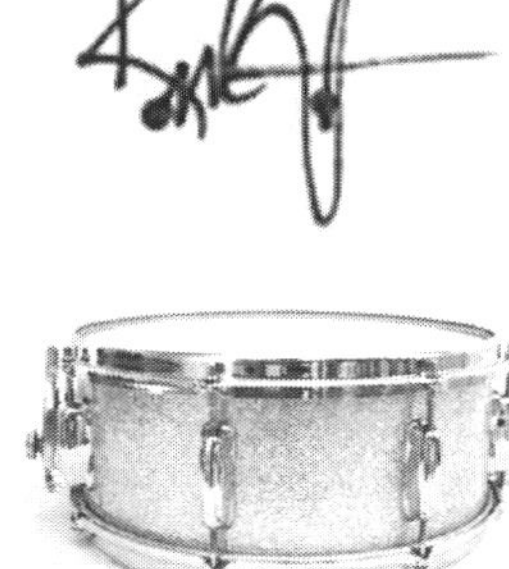

Practice Tips

In order to make measurable improvements in your drumming skills, you must practice daily and you must utilize your practice time effectively by focusing primarily on the areas that need the most attention.

Here are three important things to keep in mind when practicing:

1) Strike your playing surface using both a wrist and an arm motion.

2) Strive to make each stick go straight down and come straight up with each stroke.

3) Listen intently as you practice and strive for a smooth, steady and even execution, as if you were using only one stick.

Additionally:

4) Start practice with the **Warm-Ups** exercises and start slow!

5) Use a metronome and start with the recommended tempo markings, where indicated, and increase speed when comfortable.

6) Use heavier sticks (on a practice pad or snare drum) such as size 2B or Vic Firth "SD1 General" models.

7) Perform each exercise several times before proceeding to the next.

8) Practice exercises at soft, medium and loud volumes.

How to Use this Book

This is a workbook. Therefore, there is no particular order in which the exercises in this book must be played. Here are suggestions and additional ways for playing each of the sections:

Warm-Ups

It is not required to perform this section in its entirety. It is suggested, however, that what I call the "90° Bounce" be performed at the start of each practice session. Play each VAMP exercise several times; then, proceed to the next exercise without stopping. Alternatively, play each exercise once and proceed down the page without repeats, without stopping.

Expanding Accents and Rhythms with Rudiments

Using only the right-hand leads, play each exercise two to four times and proceed to the next exercise without stopping. Then do the same with the left-hand leads. Alternatively, play each exercise once and proceed down the page without repeats, without stopping.

Combinations

Play down the left columns only (right-hand lead), play down the right columns only (left-hand lead) and play across–left to right–for each line.
Additionally, combine two rhythms from the RHYTHM CHART, for a particular grouping, to create additional and more challenging patterns. You can also apply these exercises on the drumset by substituting a foot for one hand or both feet for both hands.

Warm-Ups

Here are the starting exercises for **STICK IT TO YOUR CHOPS**. The first exercise is the "90° Bounce." It is most effective when played VERY SLOWLY. The down stroke should be strong, allowing for more bounce. Both sticks should come up to equal heights, close to 90°. Play each line several times before proceeding to the next.

The VAMPS exercises that follow help to develop a consistent and even stroke. Play each exercise several times before proceeding to the next.

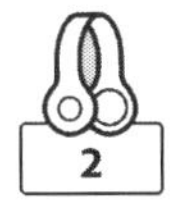

The 90° Bounce

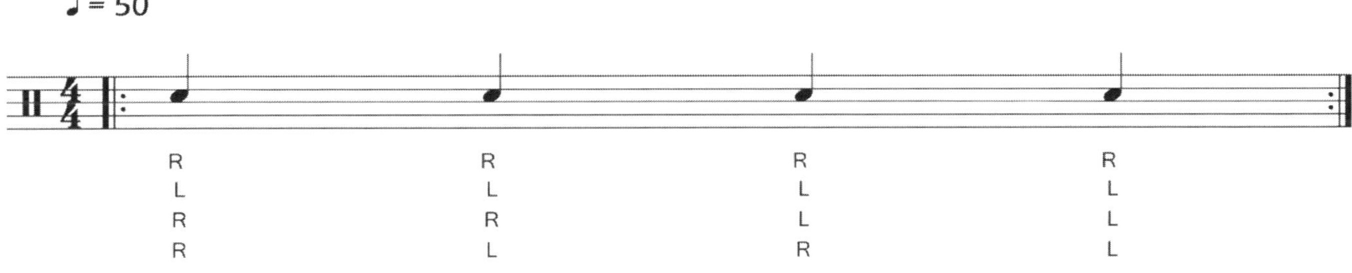

Warm-Ups

- VAMPS -

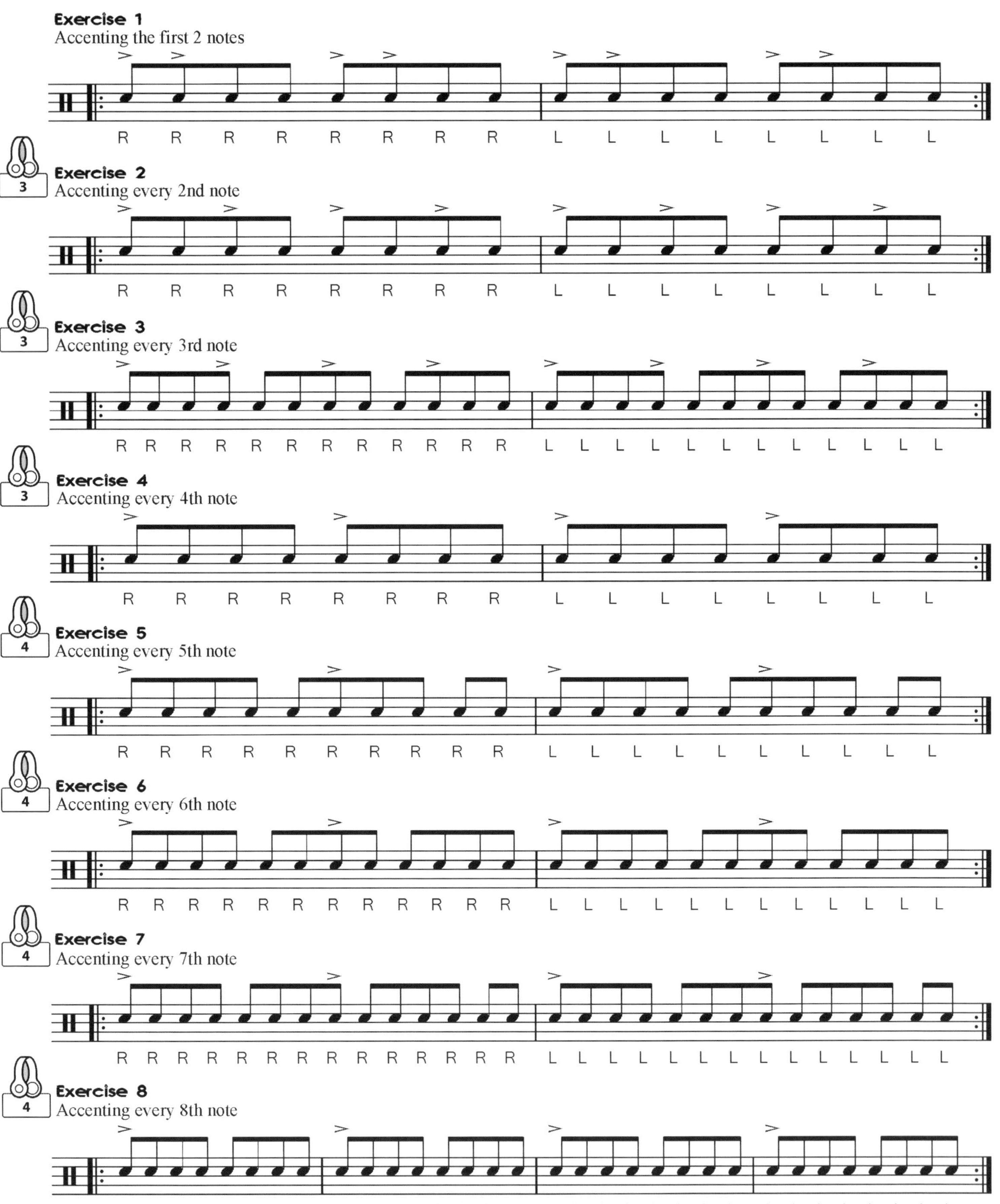

Warm-Ups

- VAMPS -

This portion contains 8th notes, grouped deliberately in 2s, 3s, 4s, etc., to illustrate various placements of accents. Due to the change in meter in each successive measure, meter markings have been omitted for simplicity.

5

Exercise 9

One stroke is successively added to each hand, up to 4 stokes, then reduced back to 1 per hand.

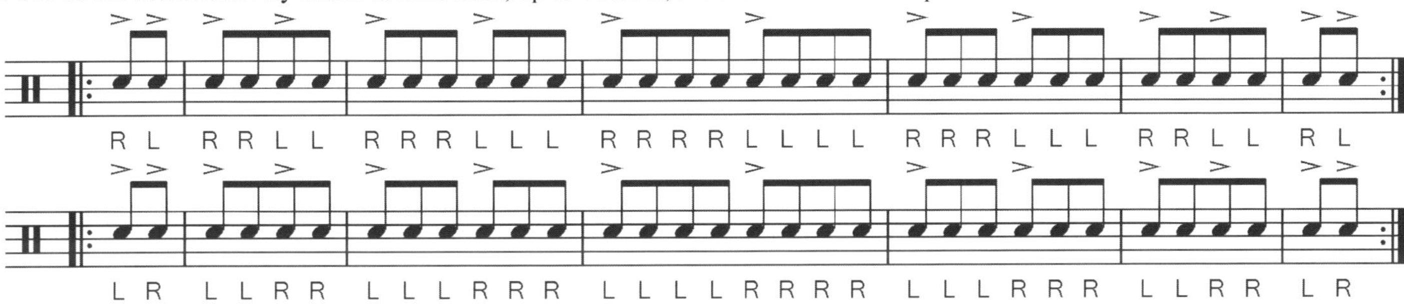

6

Exercise 10

One stroke is successively added to each hand, up to 8 stokes, then reduced back to 1 per hand.

R L R R L L R R R L L L R R R R L L L L R R R R R L L L L L R R R R R R L L L L L L

R R R R R R R L L L L L L L R R R R R R R R L L L L L L L L

R R R R R R R L L L L L L L R R R R R R L L L L L L R R R R R L L L L L

R R R R L L L L R R R L L L R R L L R L

L R L L R R L L L R R R L L L L R R R R L L L L L R R R R R L L L L L L R R R R R R

L L L L L L L R R R R R R R L L L L L L L L R R R R R R R R

L L L L L L L R R R R R R R L L L L L L R R R R R R L L L L L R R R R R

L L L L R R R R L L L R R R L L R R L R

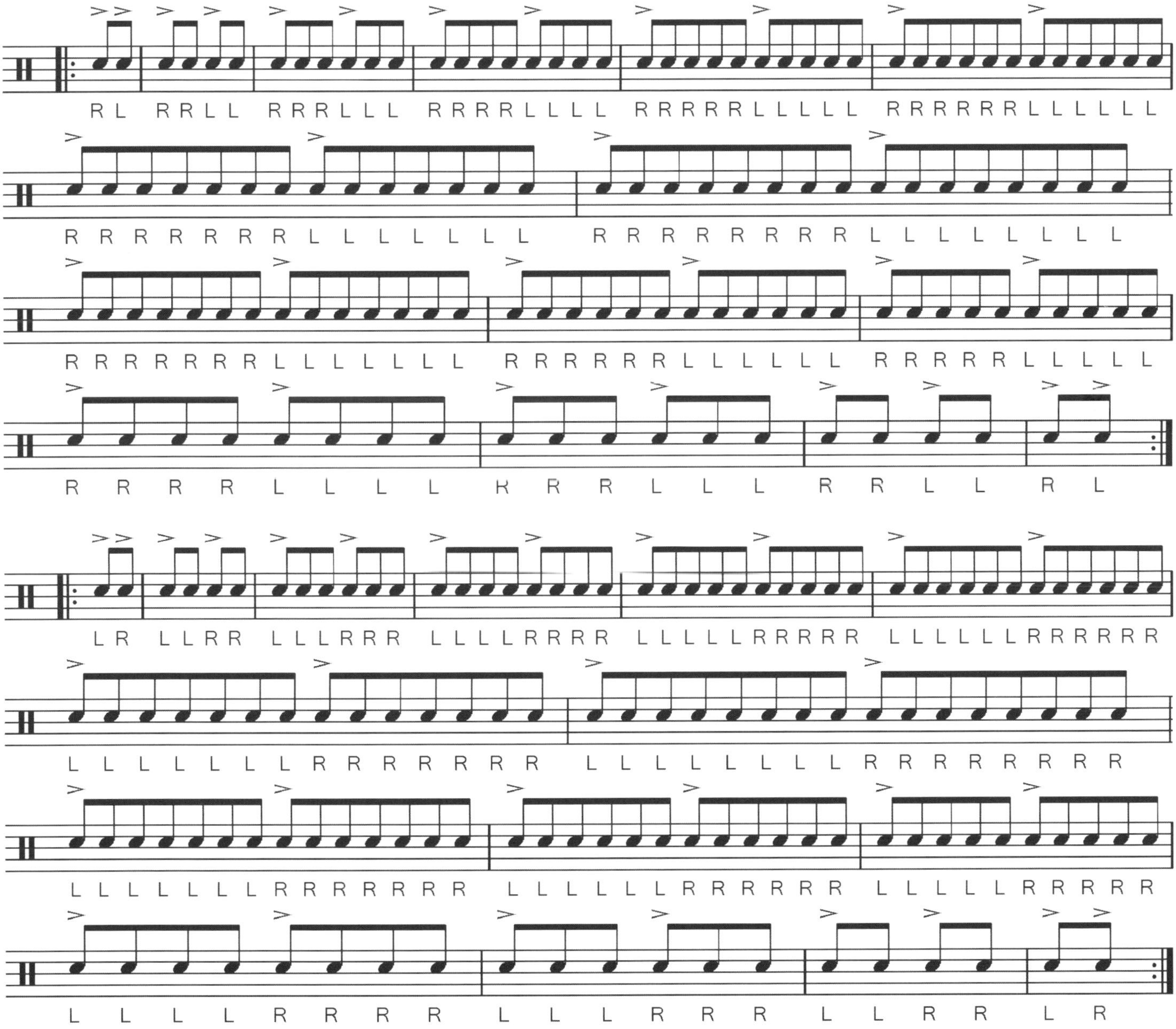

Expanding Accents and Rhythms with Rudiments

The exercises in this section employ four rudiments: the double-stroke roll, the single paradiddle, the flam tap and the flam accent. First, the double-stroke roll and the single paradiddle are grouped together in a series of exercises where accents are placed on the first two notes and in each succeeding exercise, the second accent moves one note to the right. As a result, accented notes become further and further apart; they "expand." For example, we will use Exercise 1 on page 12 (DOUBLE-STROKE ROLL). Accents are on the first two notes:

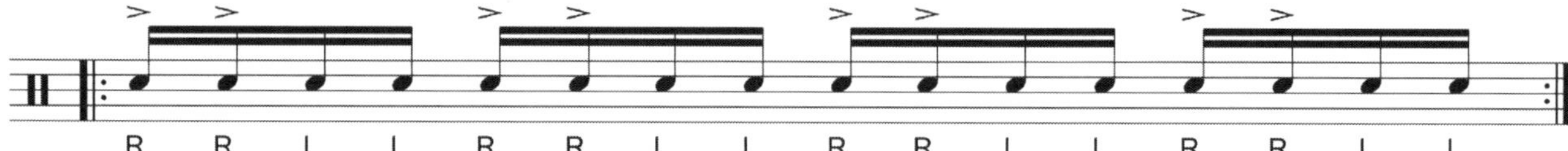

In Exercise 2, the second accent moves to the right (every other note):

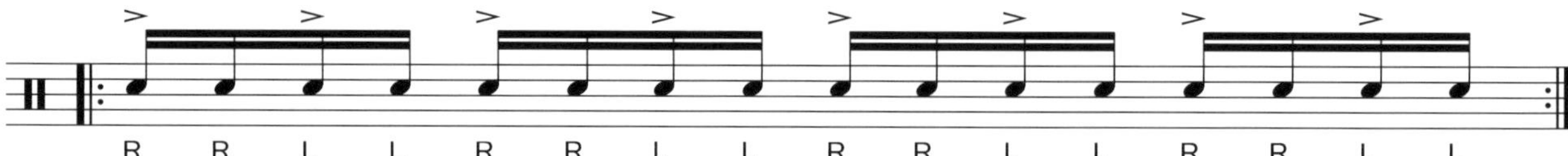

In Exercise 3, the second accent moves to every third note:

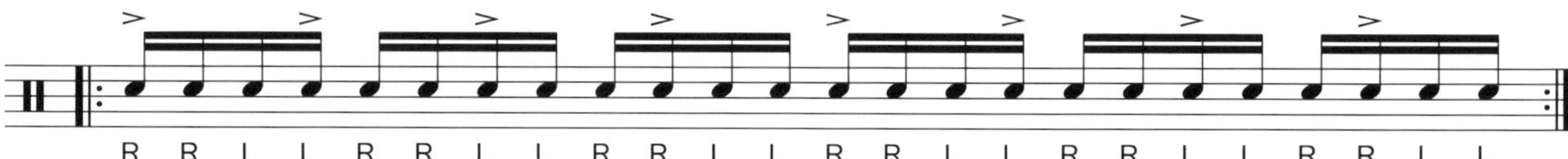

In Exercise 4, the second accent moves to every fourth note:

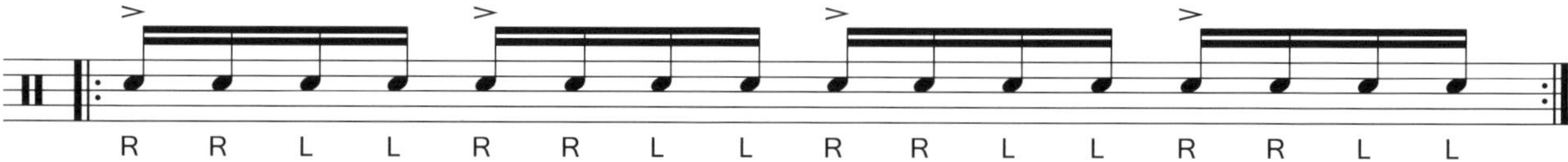

In Exercise 5, the second accent moves to every fifth note, and so on:

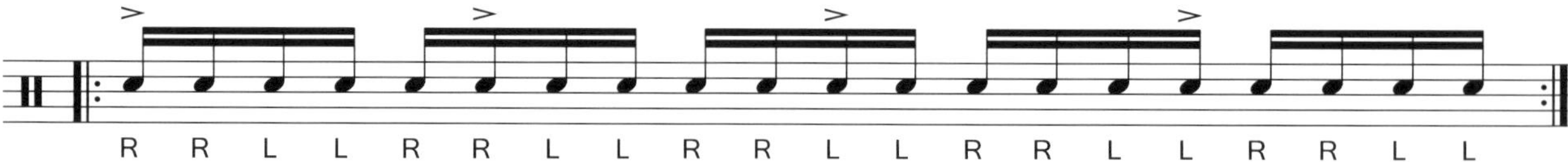

Next, the flam taps and flam accents are grouped together in exercises that "expand" sequentially as well. However, instead of an accent moving one note to the right, a flam tap or a flam accent will be added. As a result, the rhythm pattern in each succeeding exercise becomes longer. In exercises 1-8, flam taps are added, followed by one flam accent. In exercises 9-16, flam accents are added, followed by one flam tap. For example, we will use Exercise 1 on page 16–one flam tap and one flam accent:

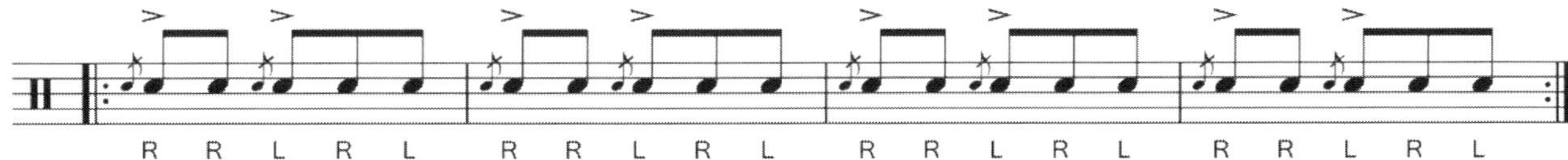

In Exercise 2, two flam taps and one flam accent:

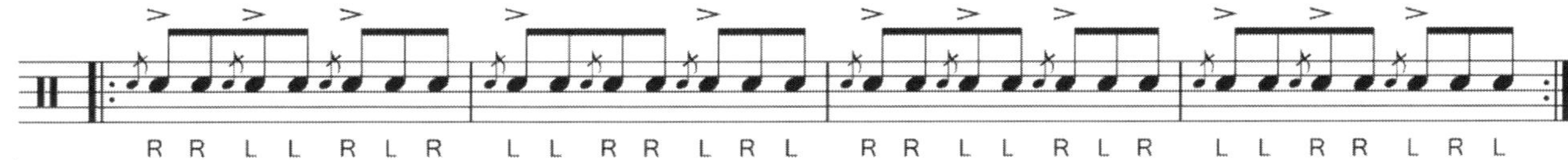

In exercise 3, three flam taps and one flam accent:

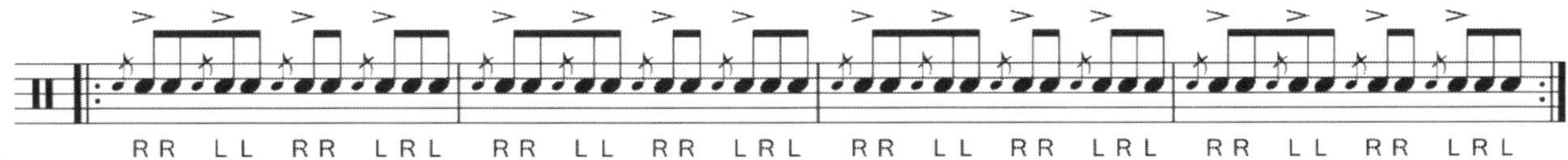

For Exercises 9-16, we follow the same process, only, we add flam accents. Exercise 9 starts with one flam accent and one flam tap:

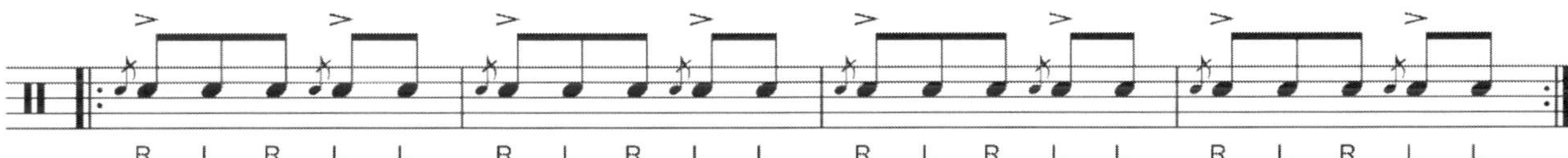

In Exercise 10, two flam accents and one flam tap:

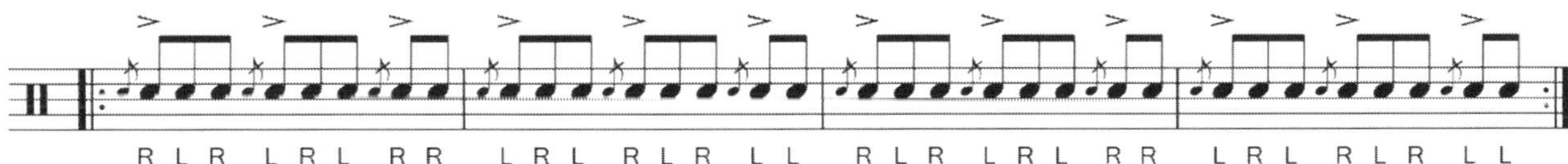

*In Exercise 11, three flam accents and one flam fap:

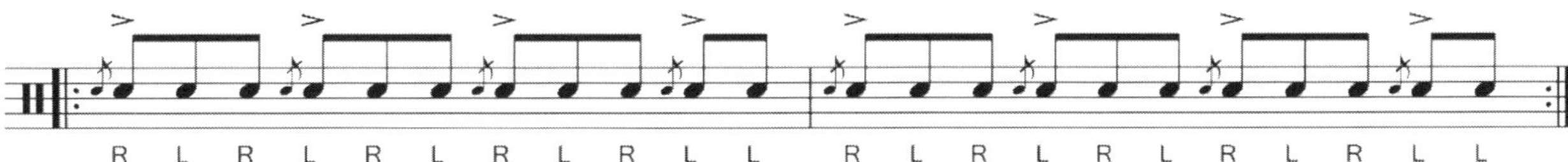

*The number of measures has been reduced to two to avoid overcrowding.

Expanding Accents and Rhythms with Rudiments

- DOUBLE-STROKE ROLL -

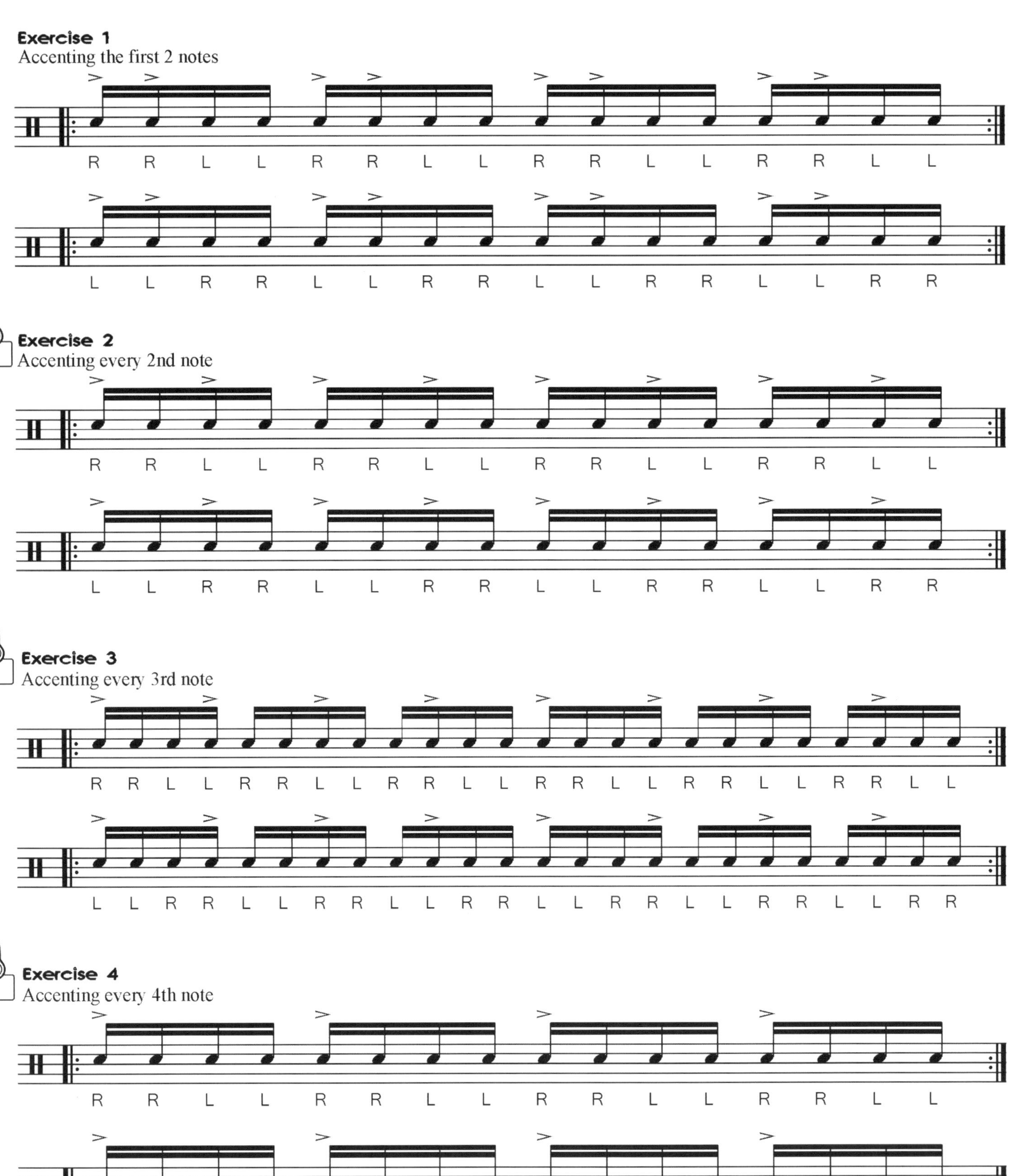

Expanding Accents and Rhythms with Rudiments

- DOUBLE-STROKE ROLL -

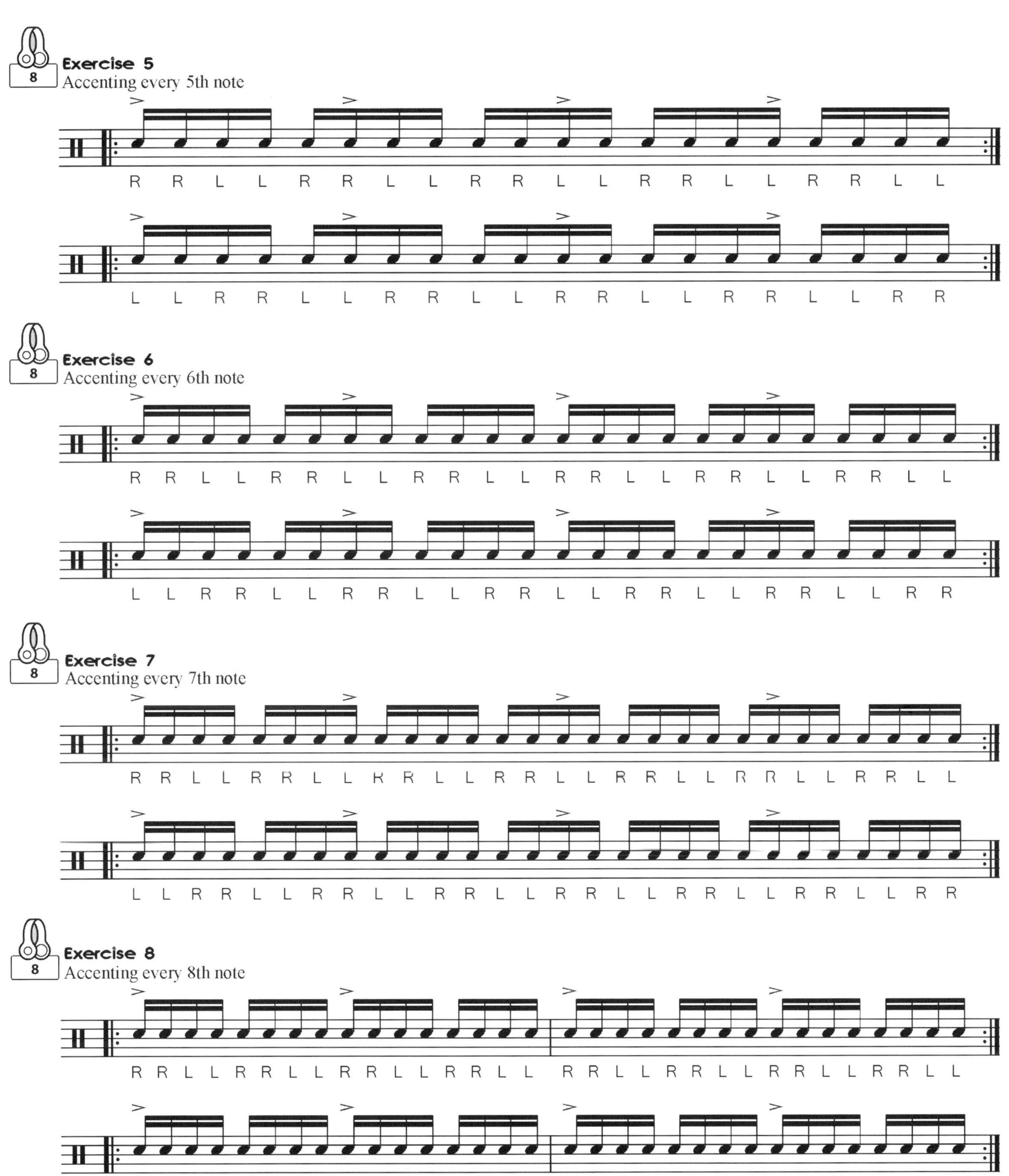

Expanding Accents and Rhythms with Rudiments

- SINGLE PARADIDDLE -

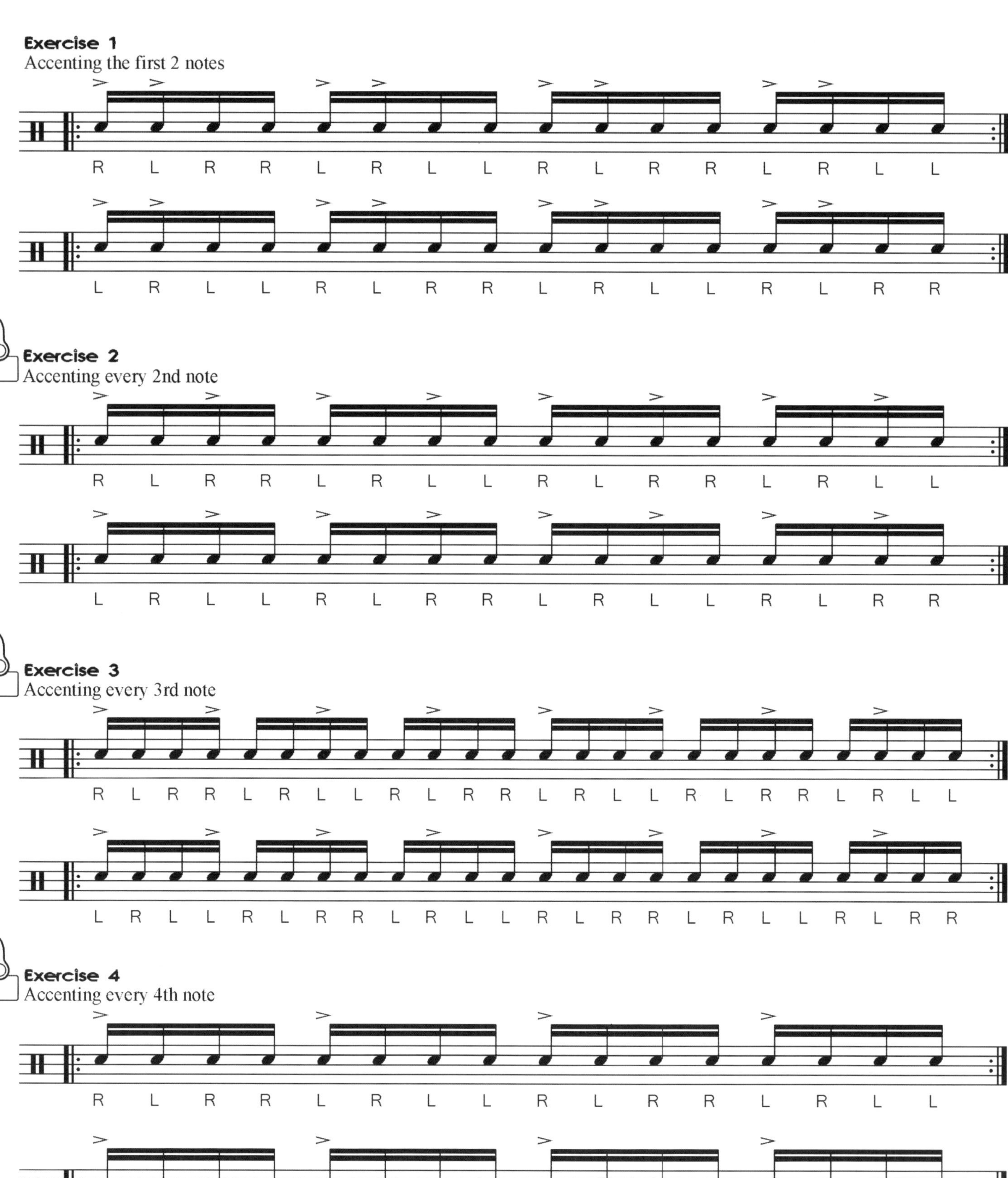

Expanding Accents and Rhythms with Rudiments

- SINGLE PARADIDDLE -

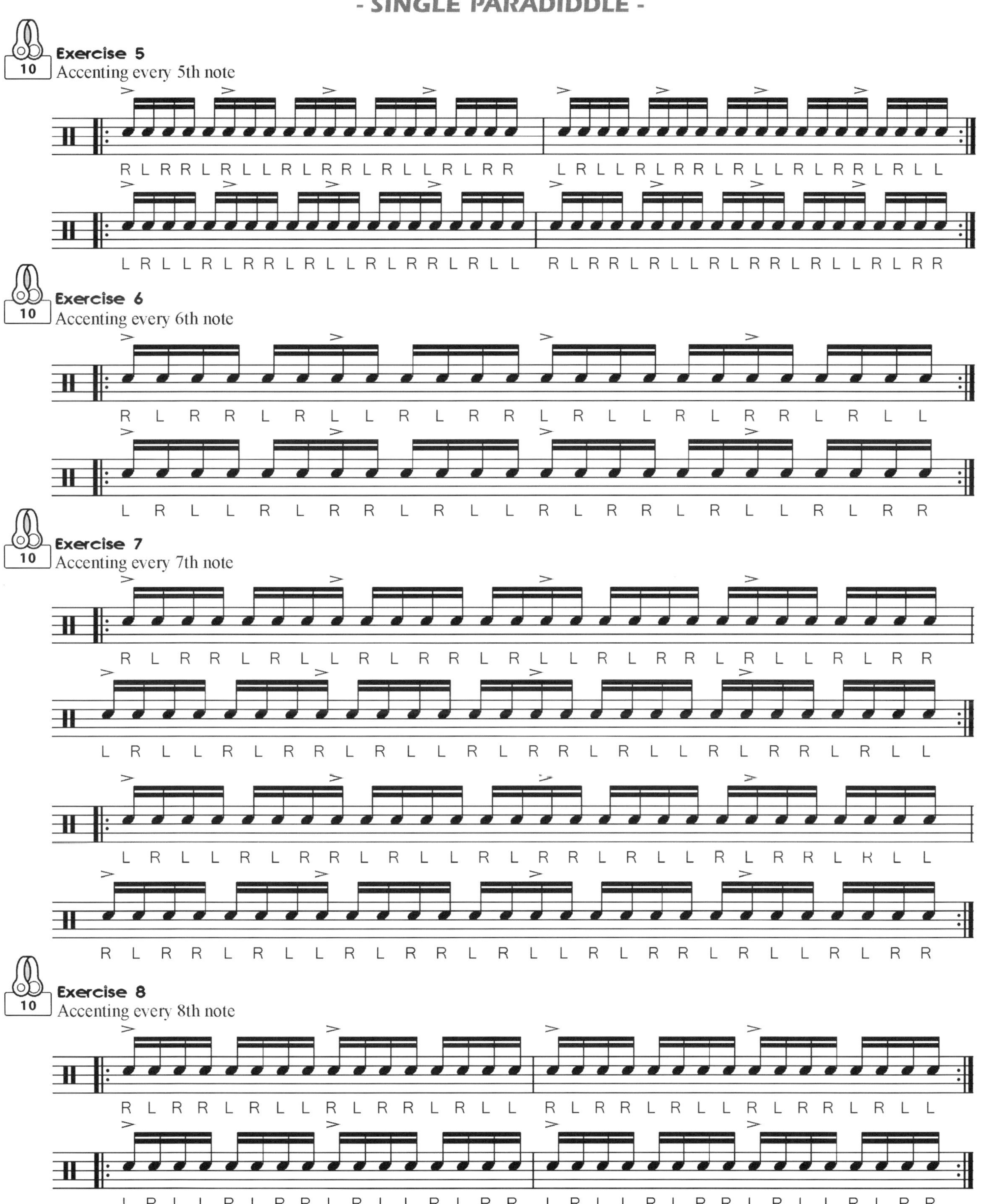

Expanding Accents and Rhythms with Rudiments

- FLAM TAPS AND FLAM ACCENTS -

Please note below that, because exercises 1, 2, 3, 9, and 10 are short in length, their amount of measures are doubled.

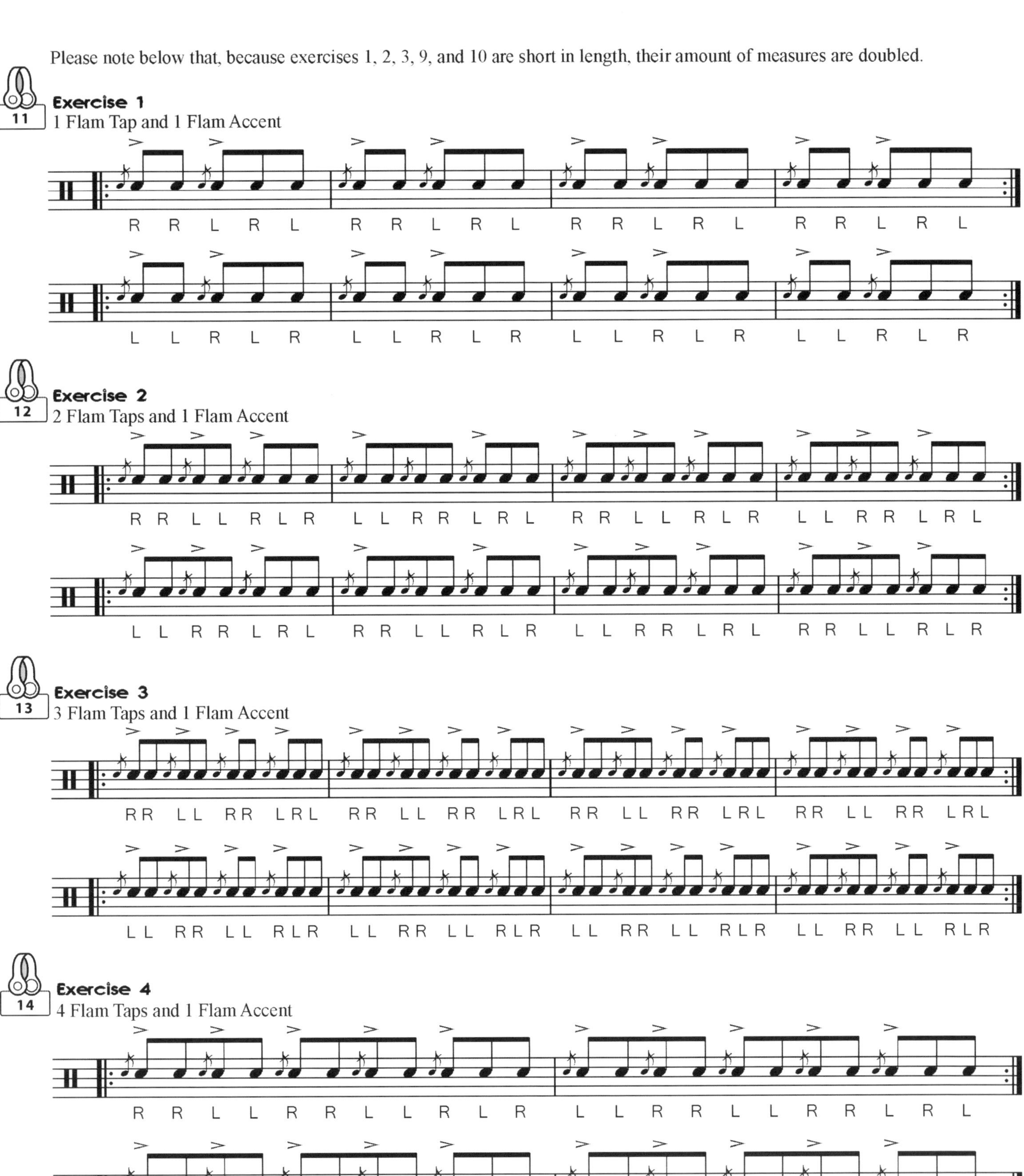

Expanding Accents and Rhythms with Rudiments

- FLAM TAPS AND FLAM ACCENTS -

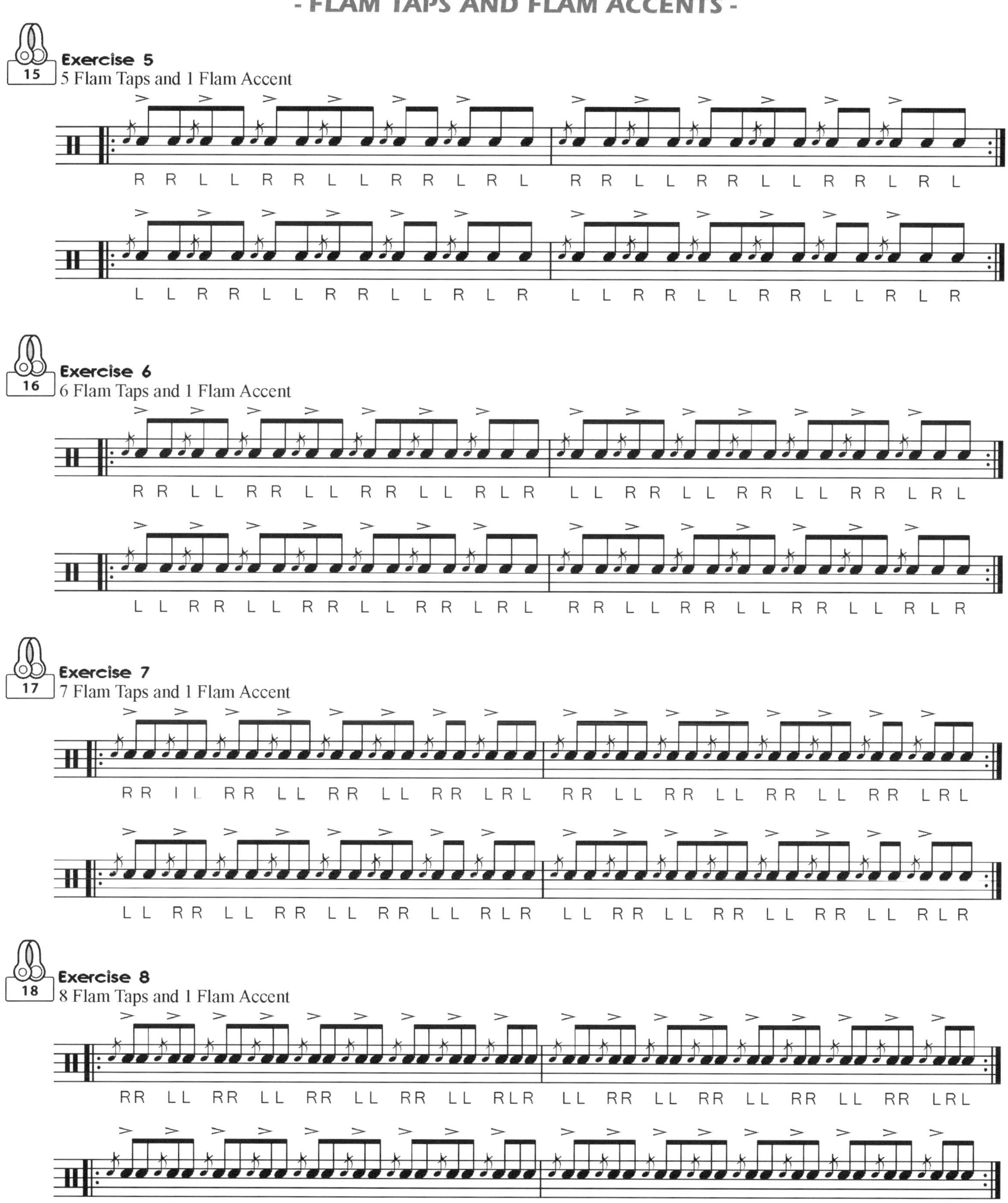

Expanding Accents and Rhythms with Rudiments

- FLAM TAPS AND FLAM ACCENTS -

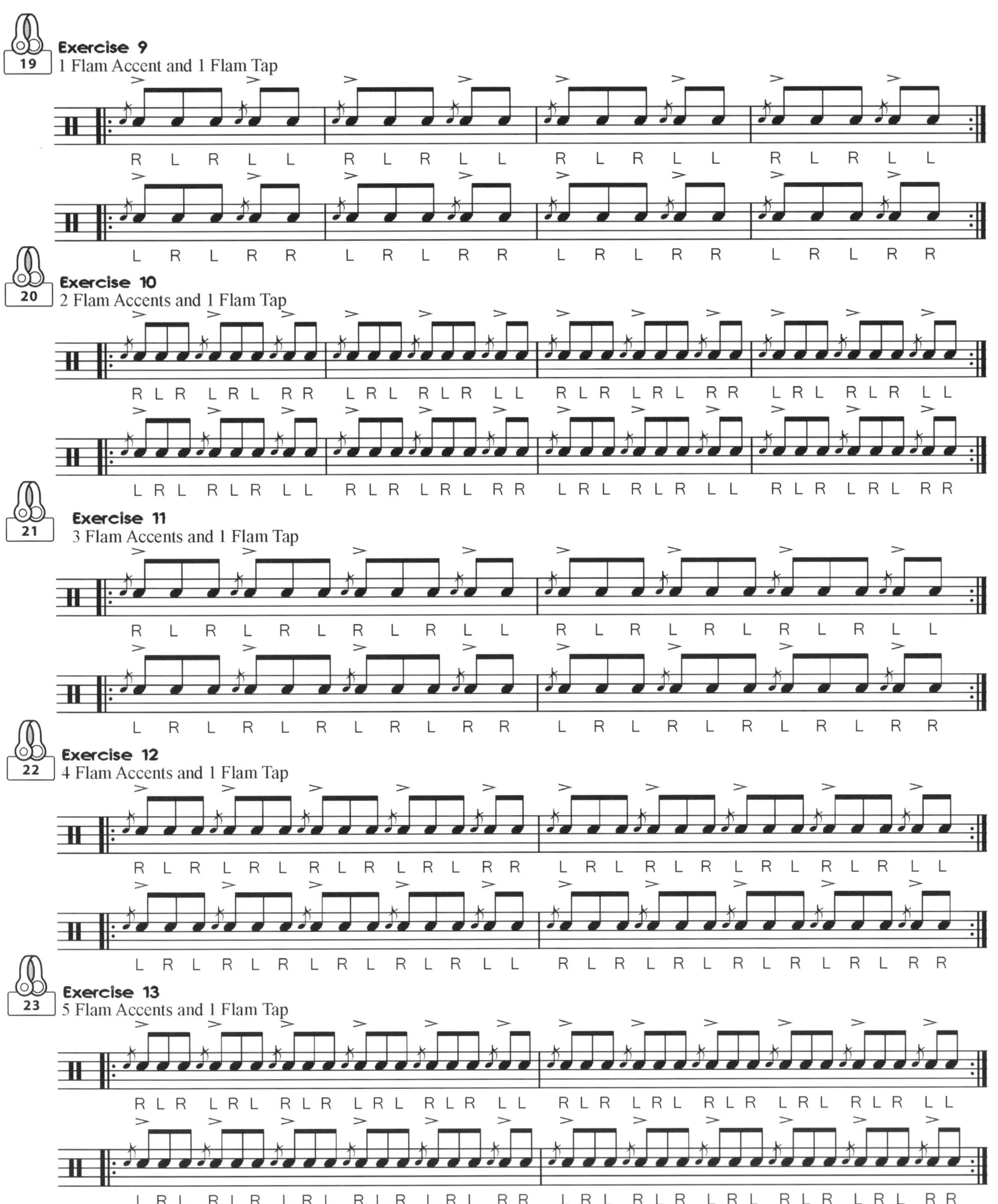

Expanding Accents and Rhythms with Rudiments

- FLAM TAPS AND FLAM ACCENTS -

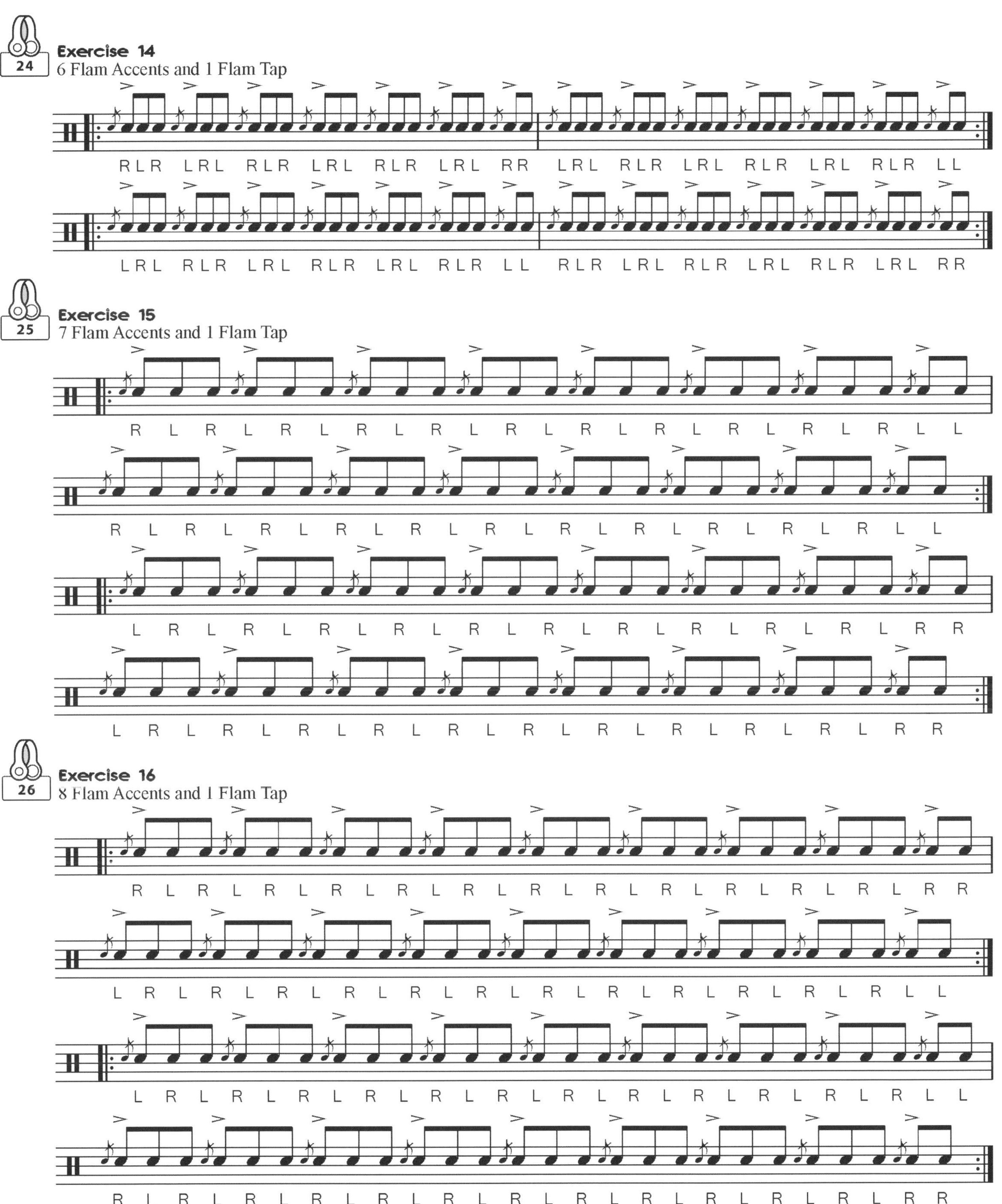

Combinations

In this section every L-R sticking combination is presented in a group of three, four, five, six, seven and eight. These exercises are great for building speed, dexterity and consistency of sound. The challenge is to make each note of the exercises sound the same, regardless of sticking. They should sound as though you're playing with only one stick.

Following each grouping is a RHYTHM CHART. The purpose of these charts is to provide a variety of additional rhythms to apply to the grouping. For example, we will select Exercise 1 from **4-note combinations** on page 22:

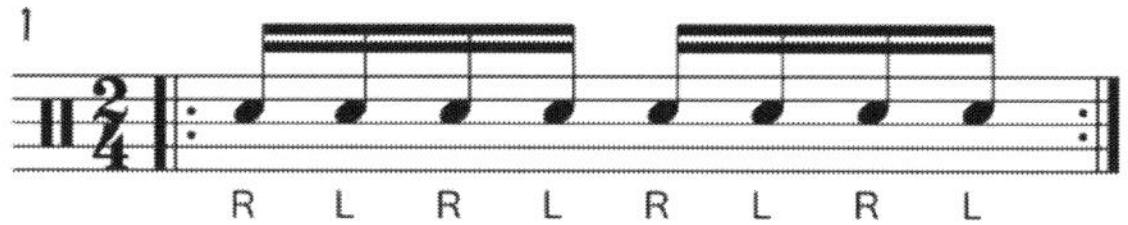

Next, we will select Rhythm #1 from the **4-Note Combinations** RHYTHM CHART on page 23:

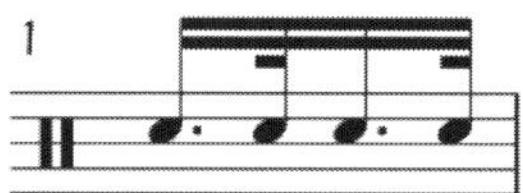

"Exercise 1" would then change to this:

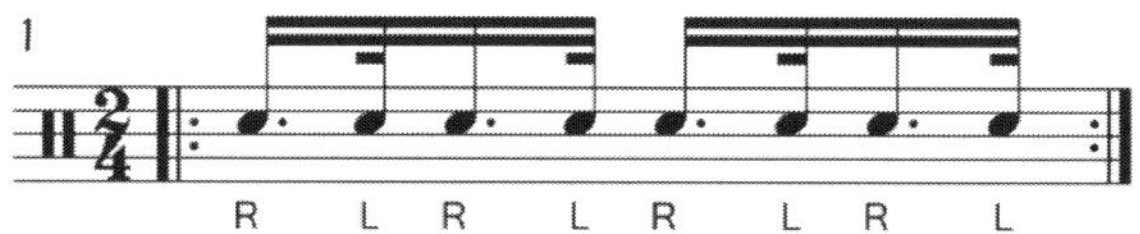

Instead of straight sixteenths, you would be playing a dotted eighth and sixteenth rhythm while observing the same L-R sticking pattern.

When you apply a rhythm from any of the RHYTHM CHARTS, you will be playing it twice, in order to keep the number of notes consistent. The combination rhythms, found in the **4-Note Combinations** RHYTHM CHART, are the exception.

For example, the **4-Note Combinations** RHYTHM CHART on page 23 contains twenty-one rhythms. Therefore, you can play each of the **4-Note Combinations** on page 22 using a total of twenty-two different rhythm patterns. As the number of notes in the combinations increases, so grows the number of possible rhythmic variations.

3-Note Combinations

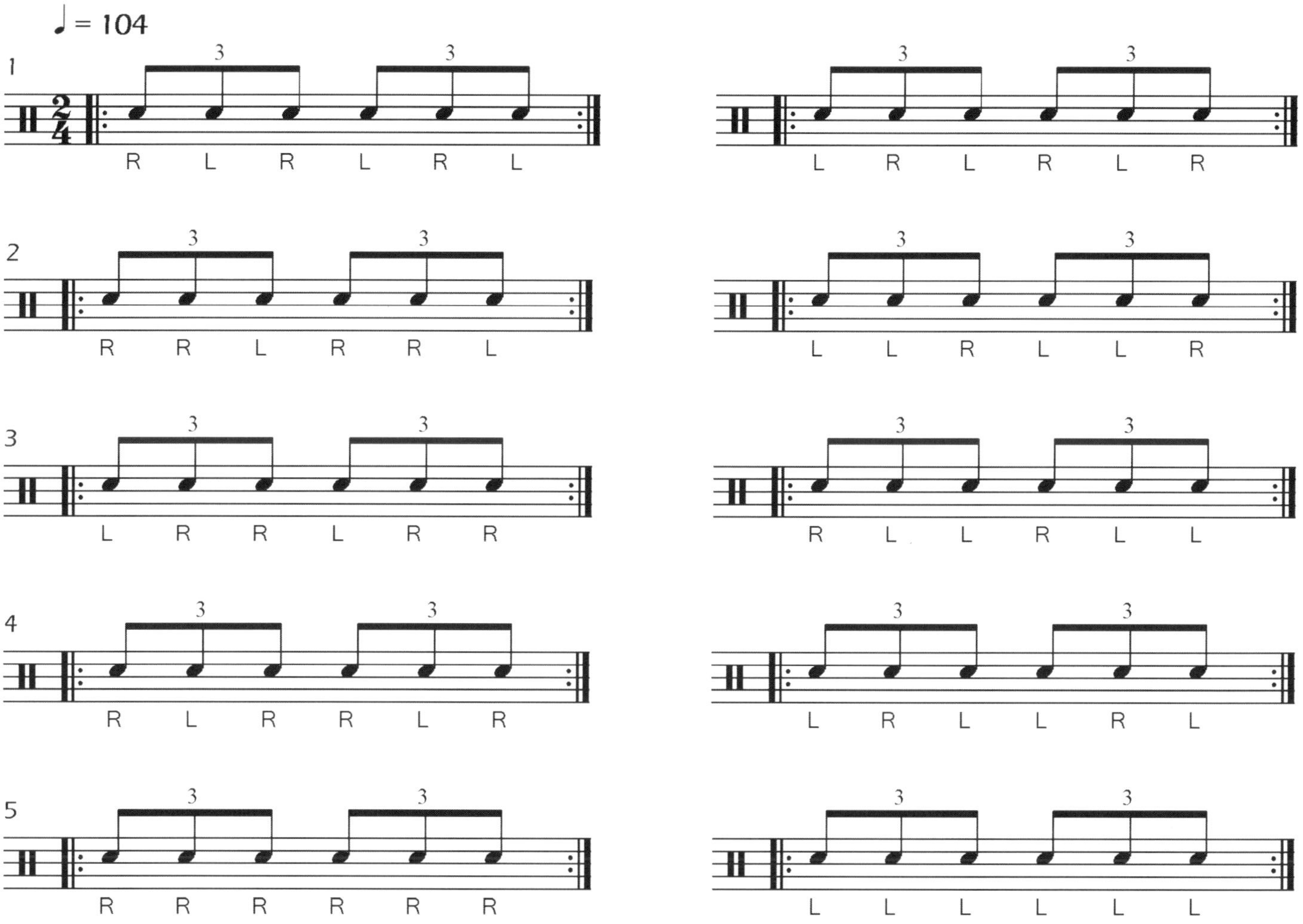

♩ = 104

1. R L R L R L — L R L R L R
2. R R L R R L — L L R L L R
3. L R R L R R — R L L R L L
4. R L R R L R — L R L L R L
5. R R R R R R — L L L L L L

3-Note Combinations

- RHYTHM CHART -

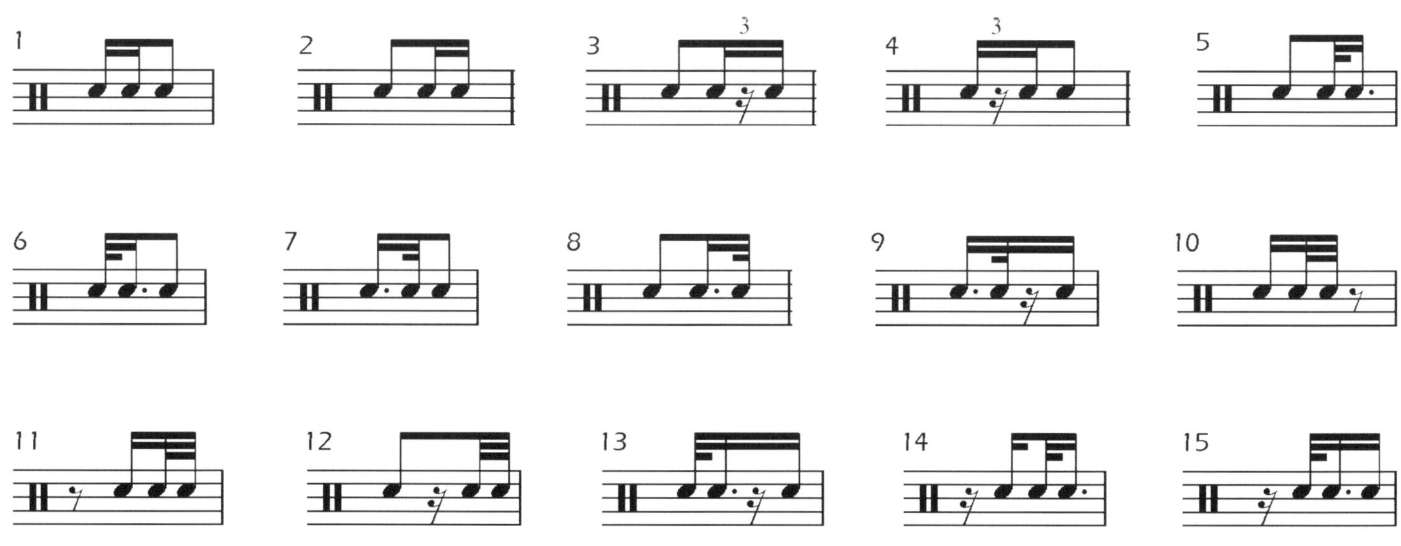

4-Note Combinations

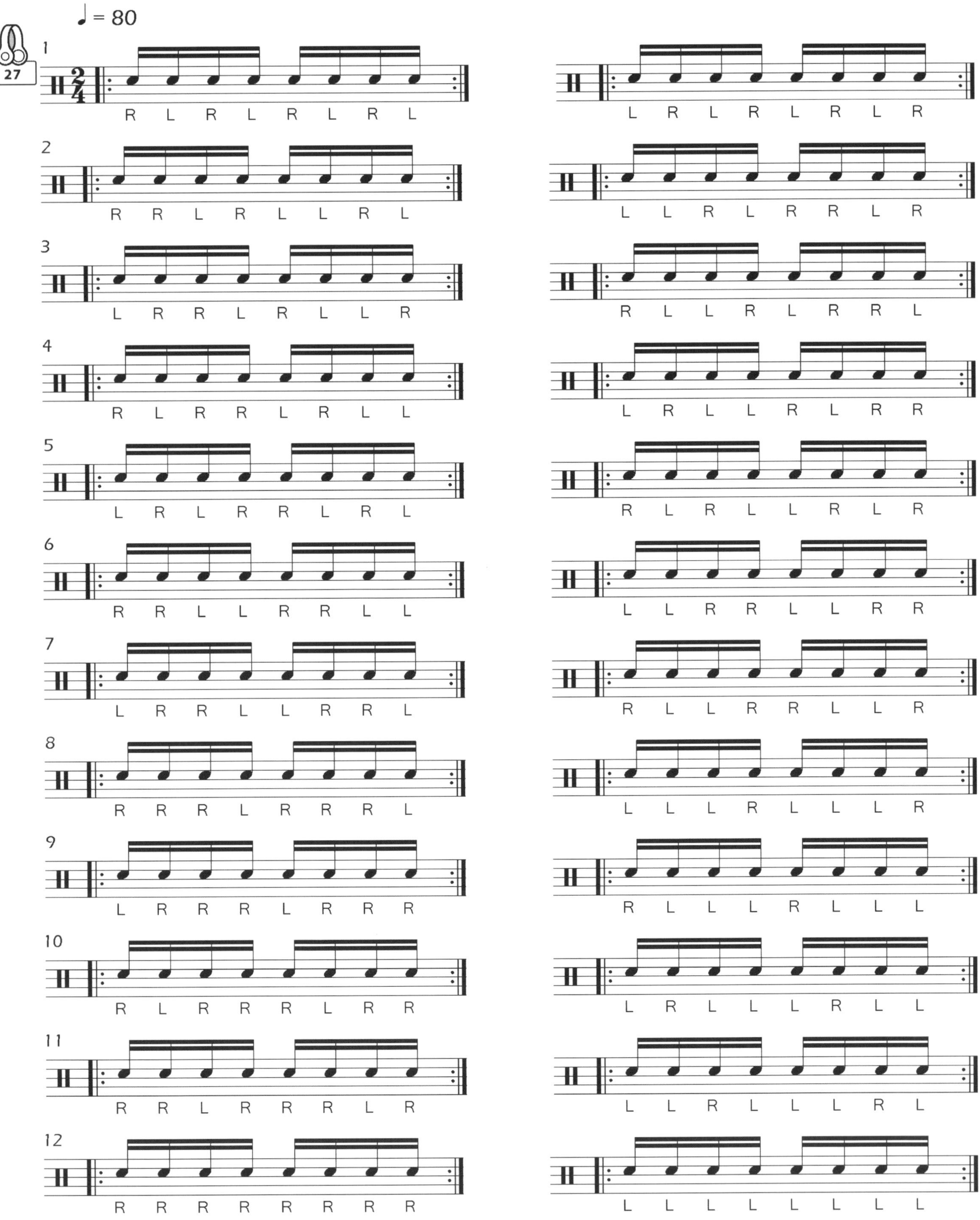

4-Note Combinations

- RHYTHM CHART -

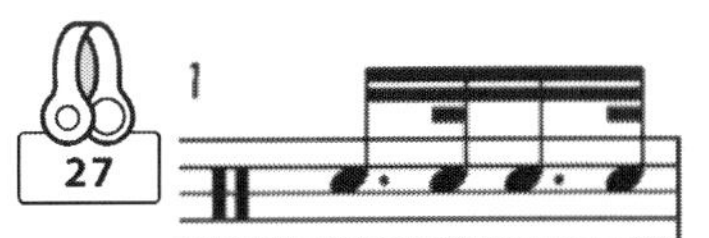

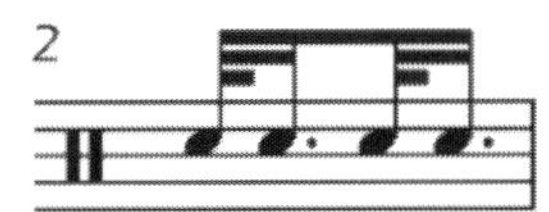

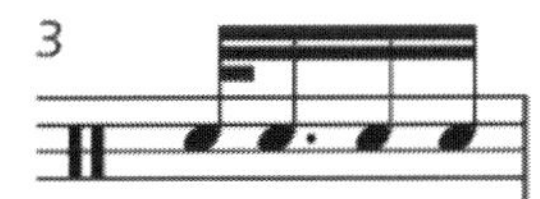

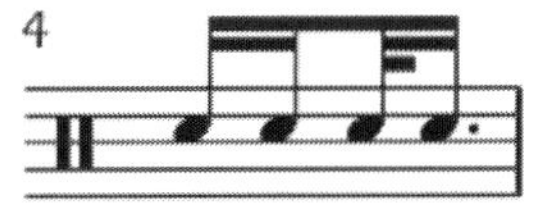

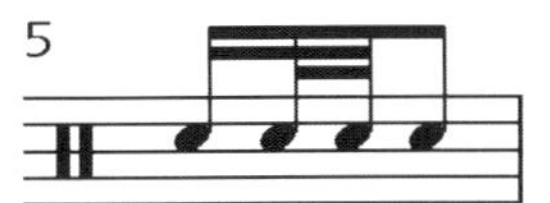

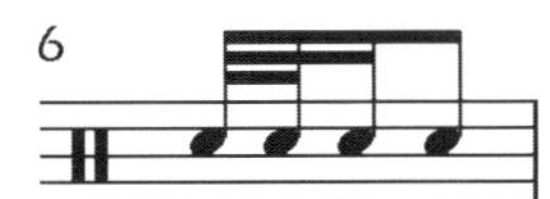

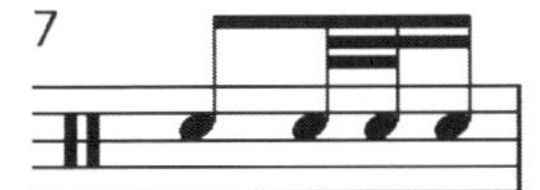

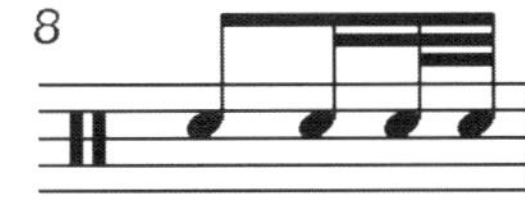

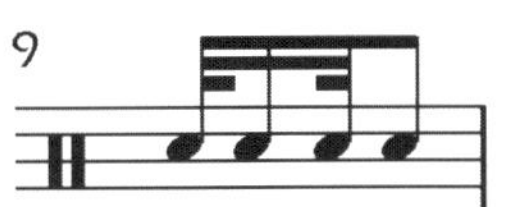

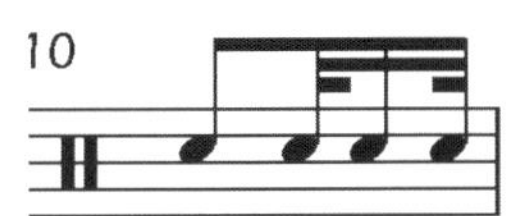

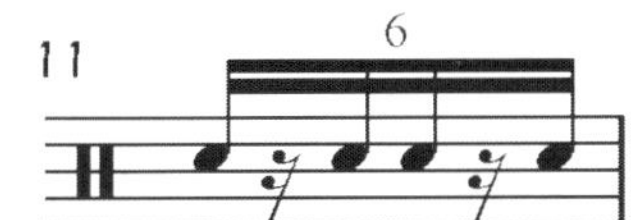

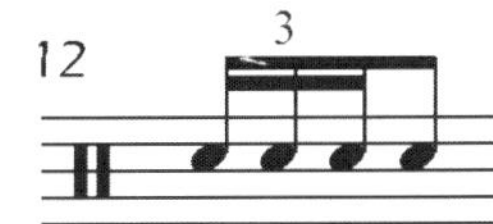

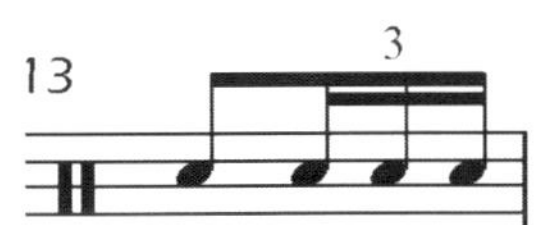

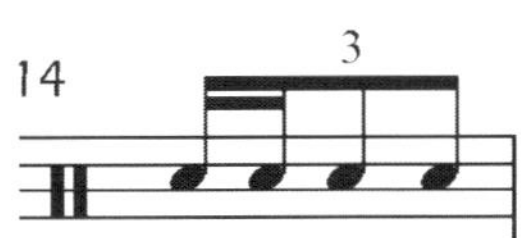

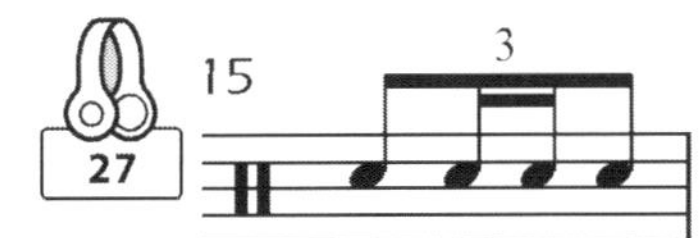

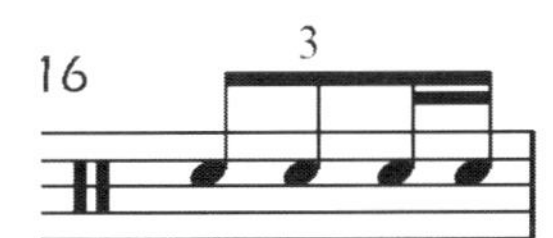

Combination Rhythms

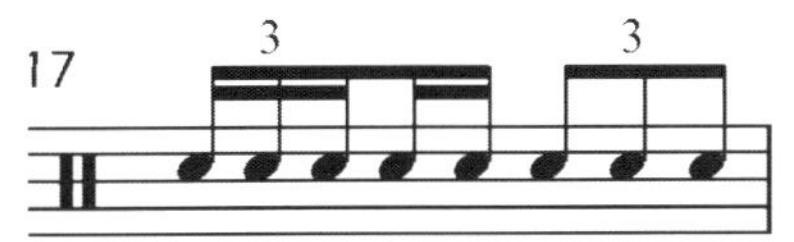

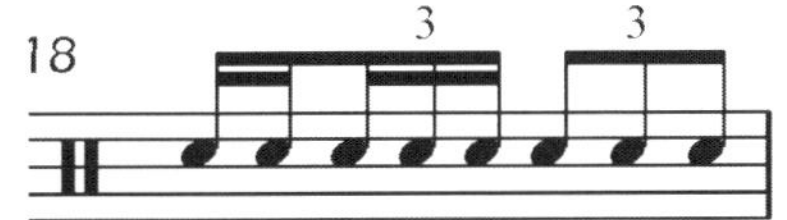

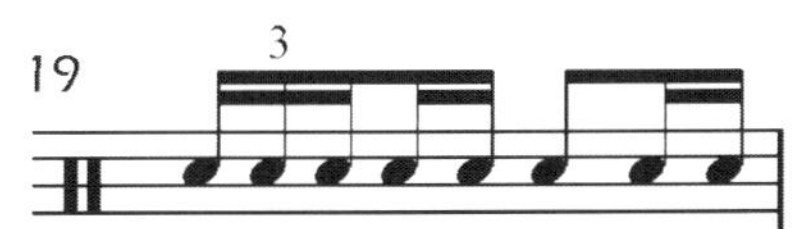

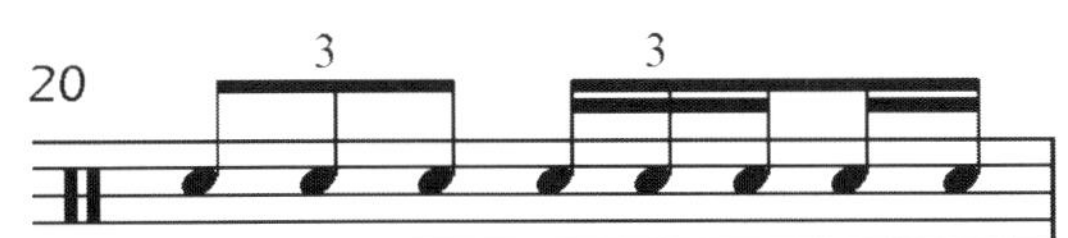

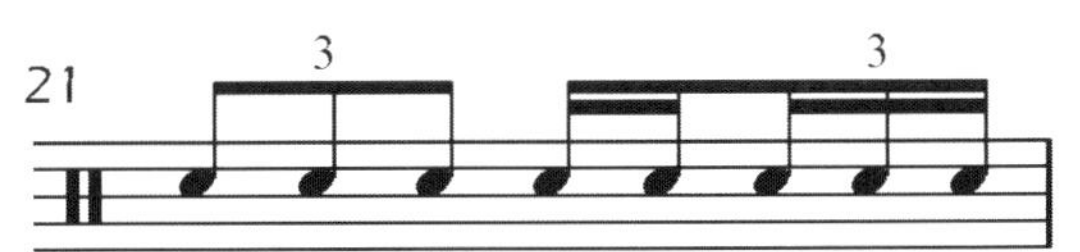

5-Note Combinations

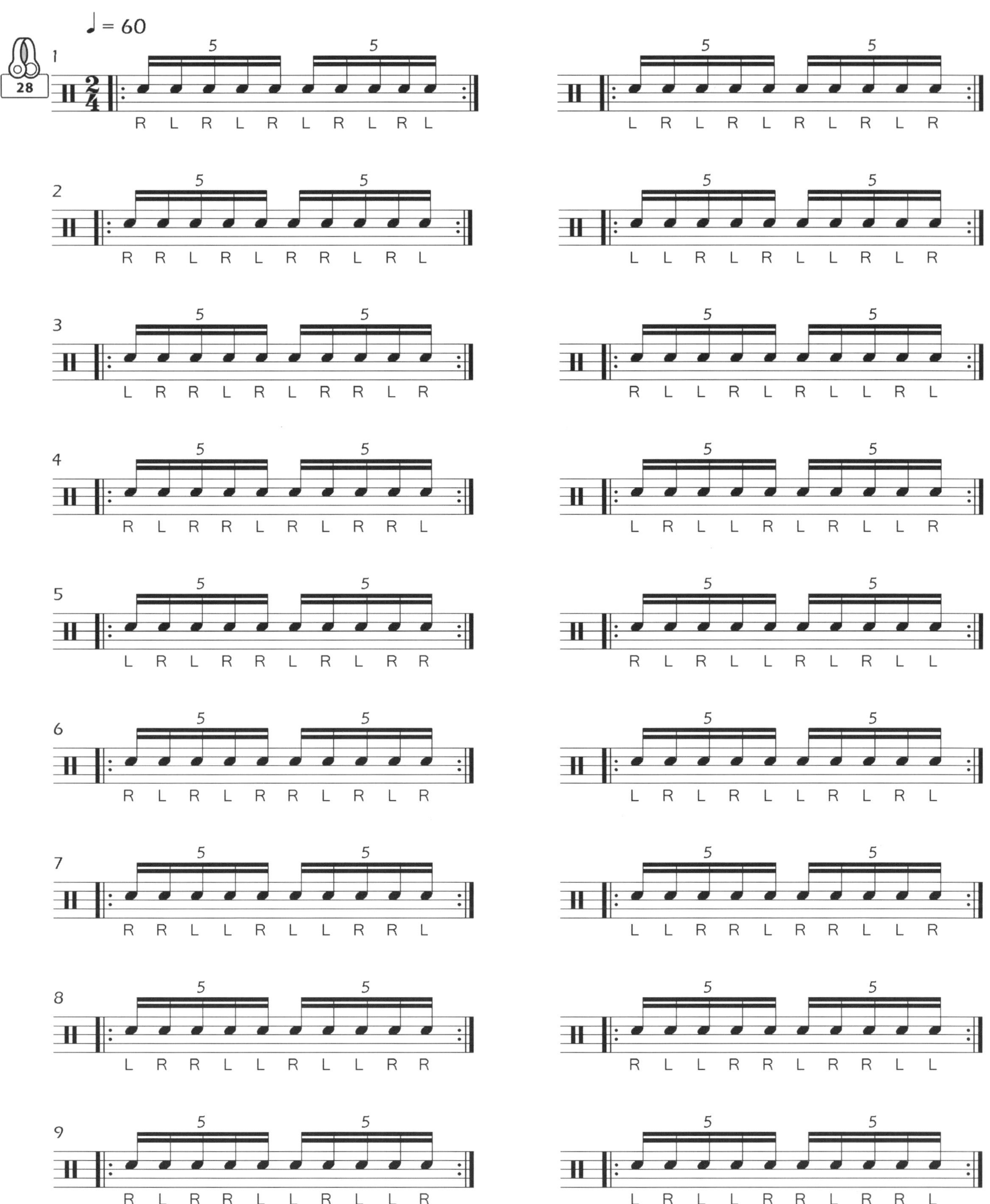

5-Note Combinations

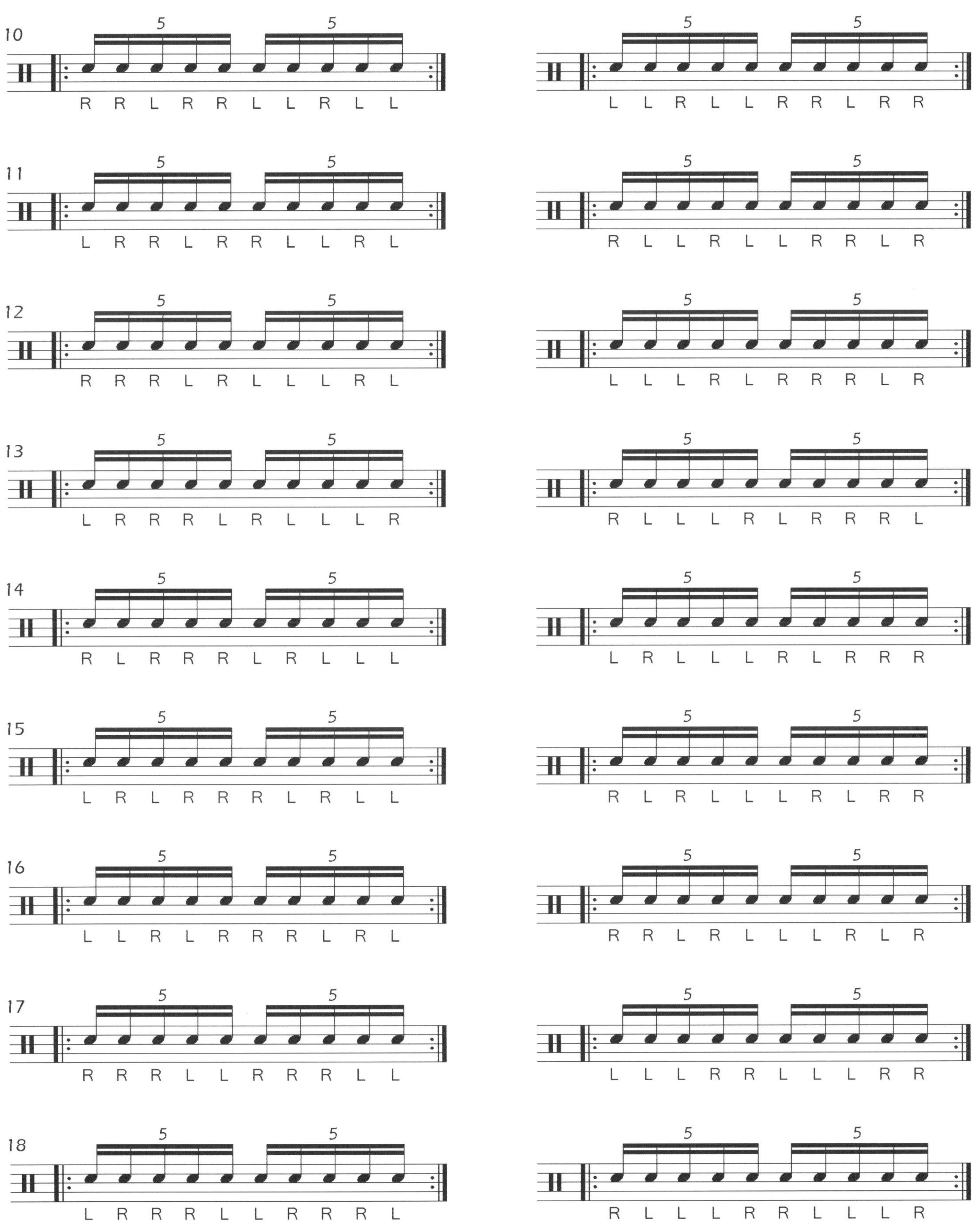

5-Note Combinations

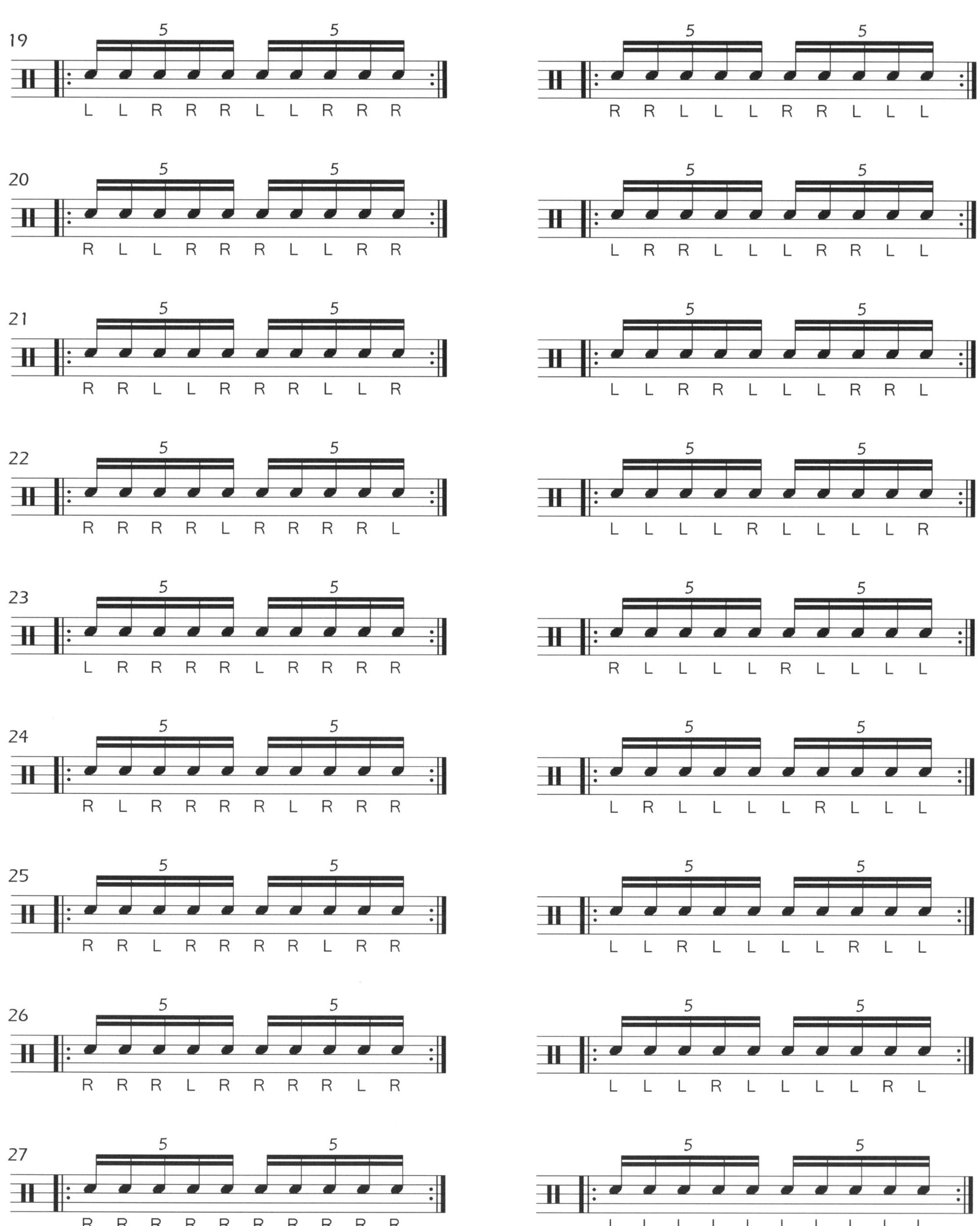

5-Note Combinations

- RHYTHM CHART -

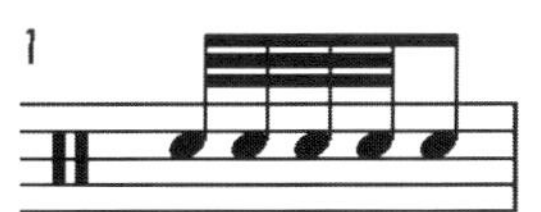

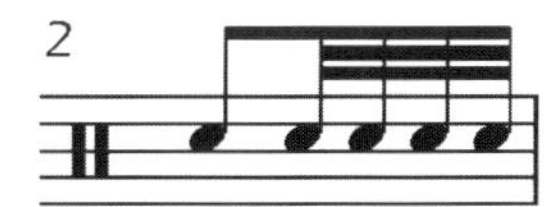

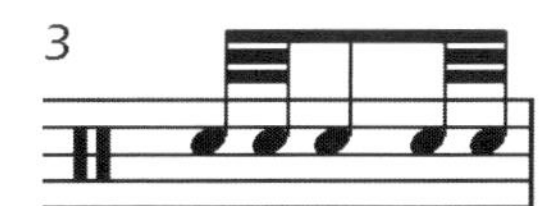

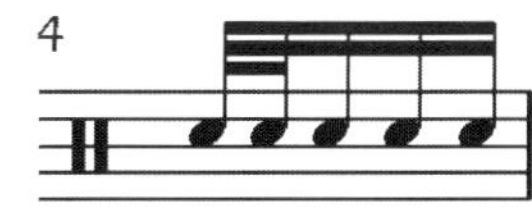

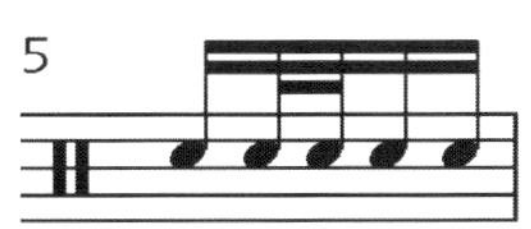

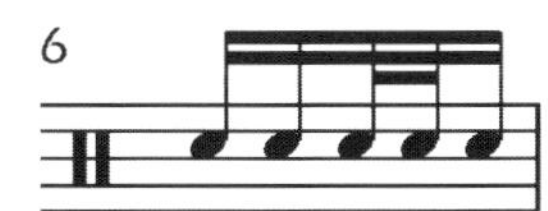

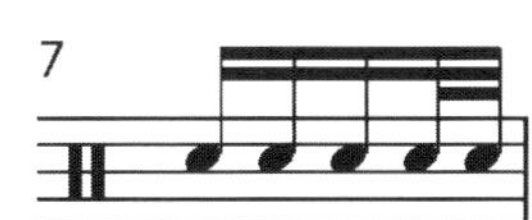

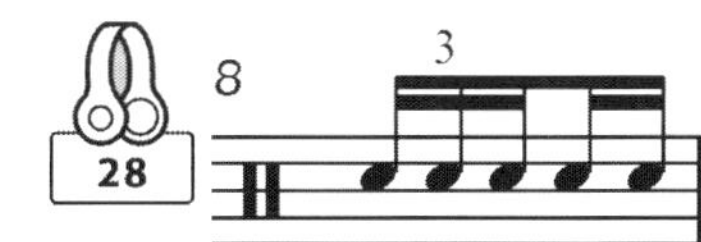

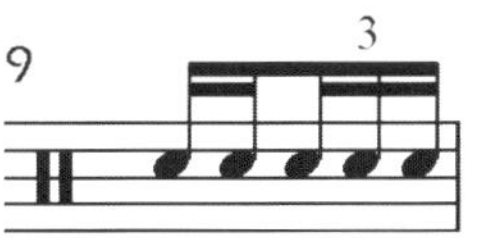

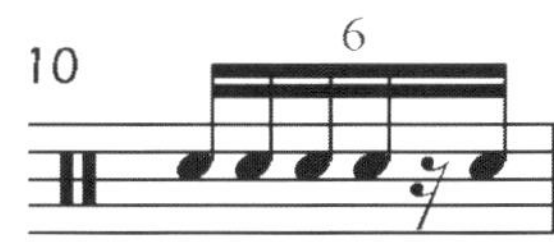

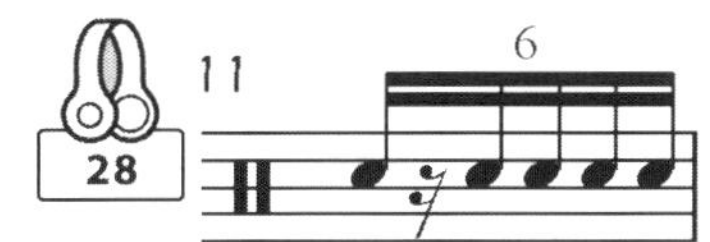

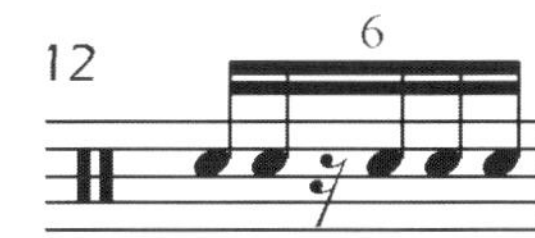

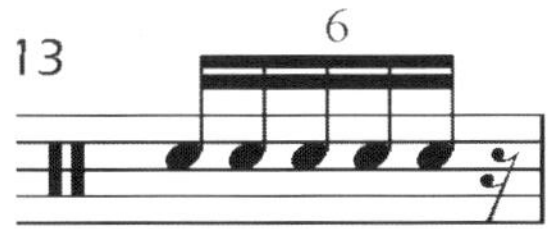

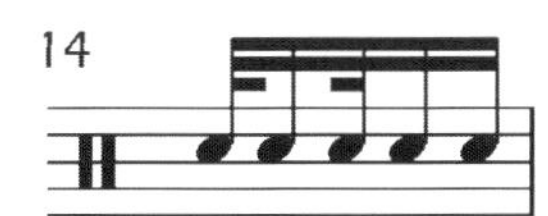

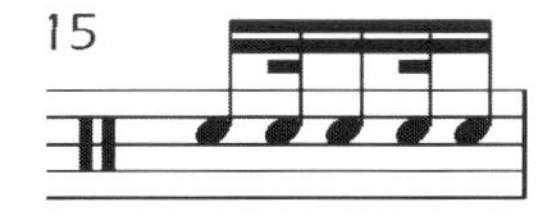

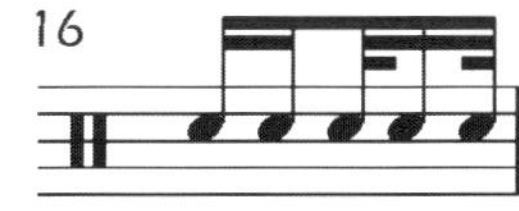

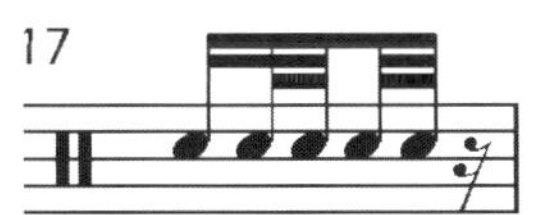

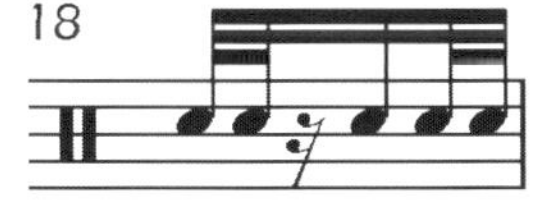

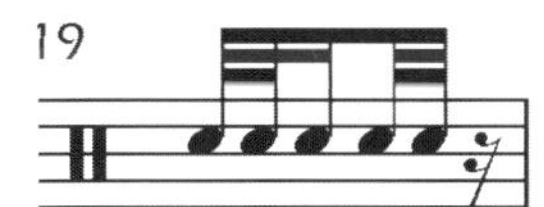

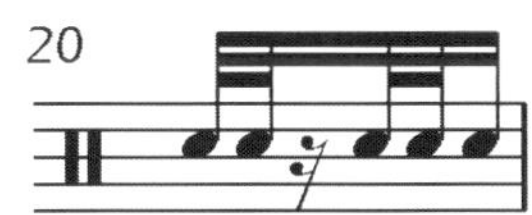

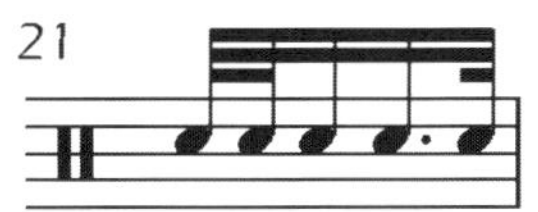

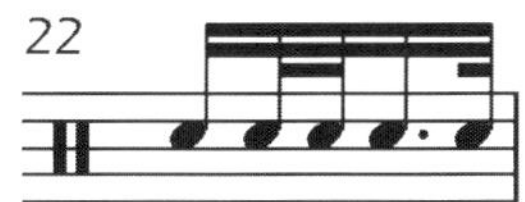

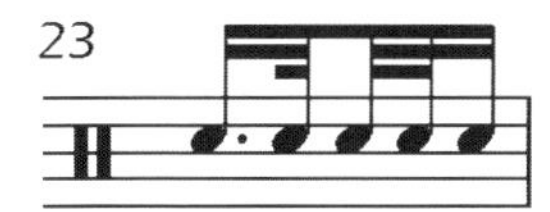

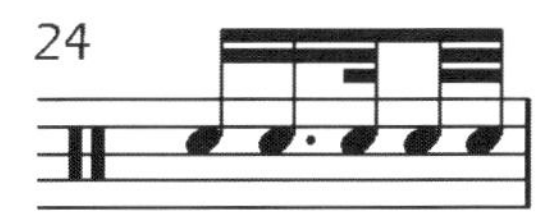

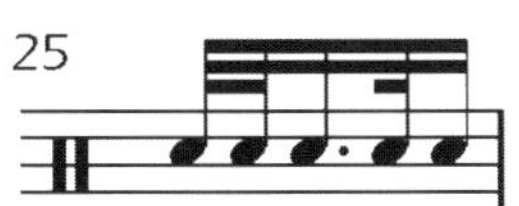

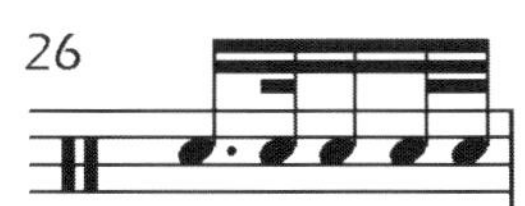

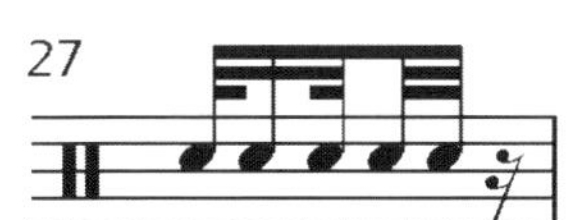

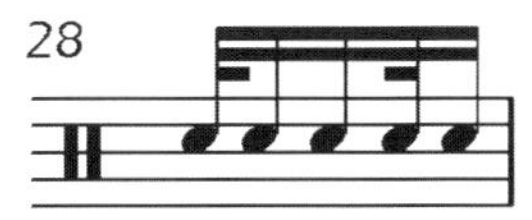

6-Note Combinations

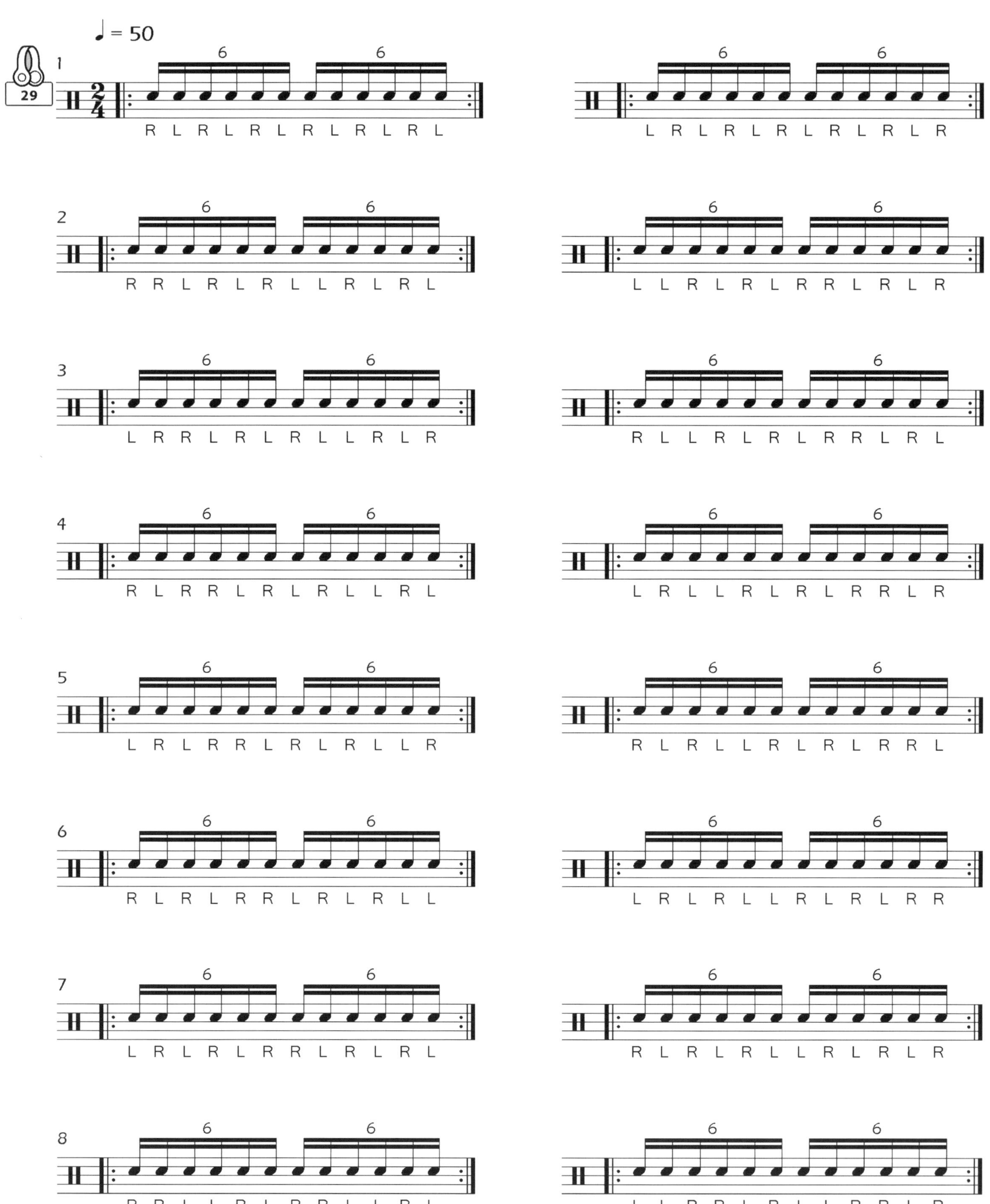

6-Note Combinations

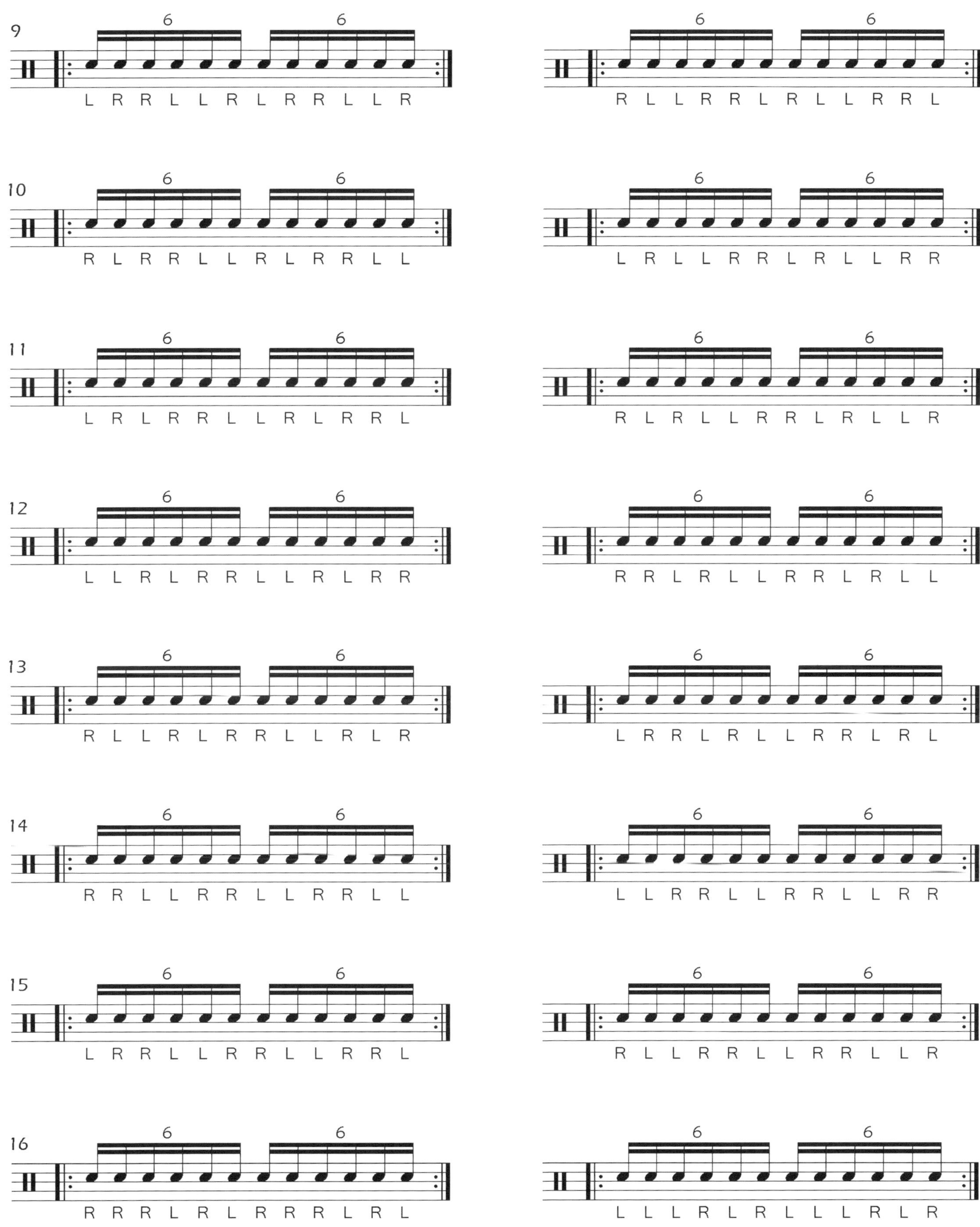

6-Note Combinations

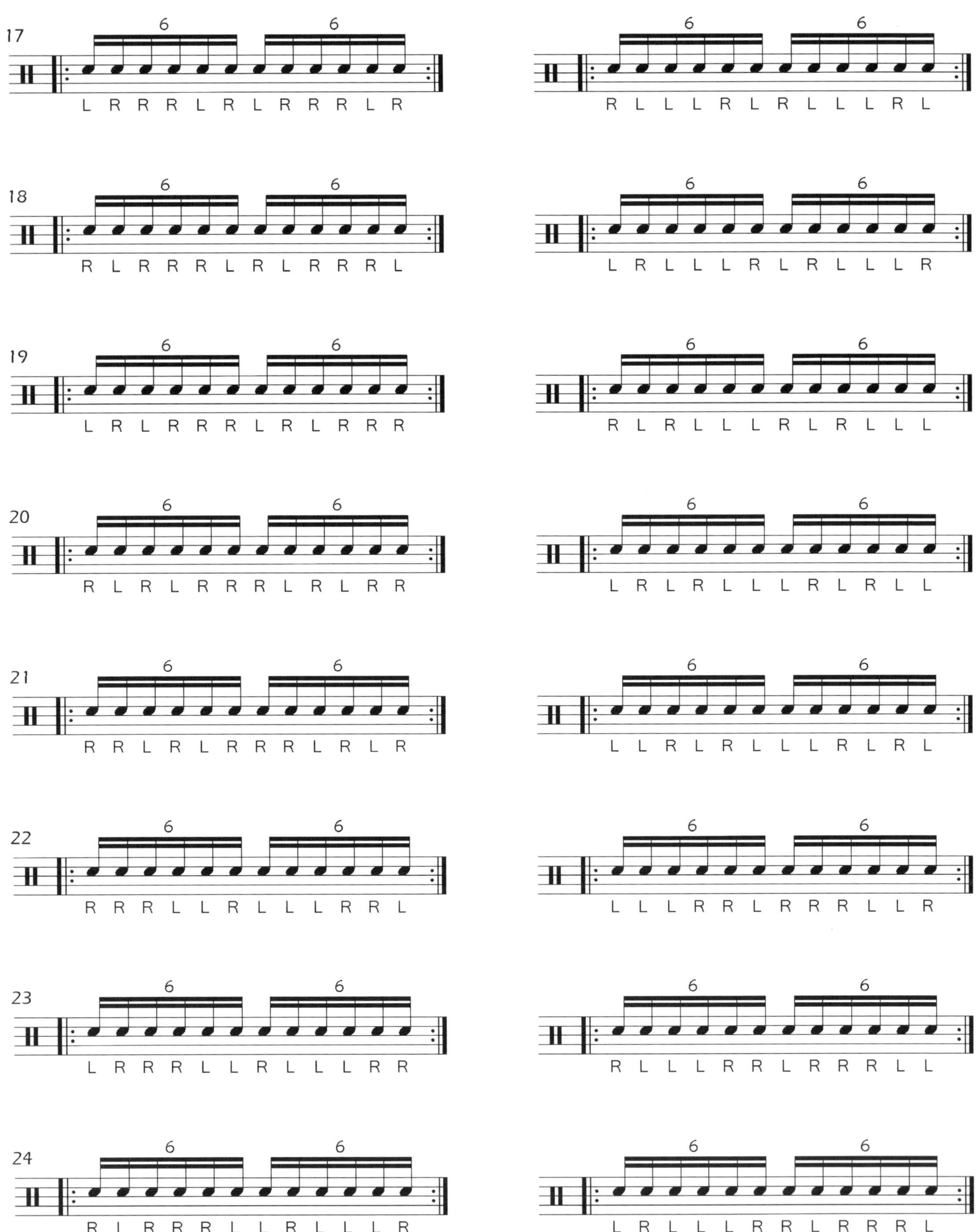

6-Note Combinations

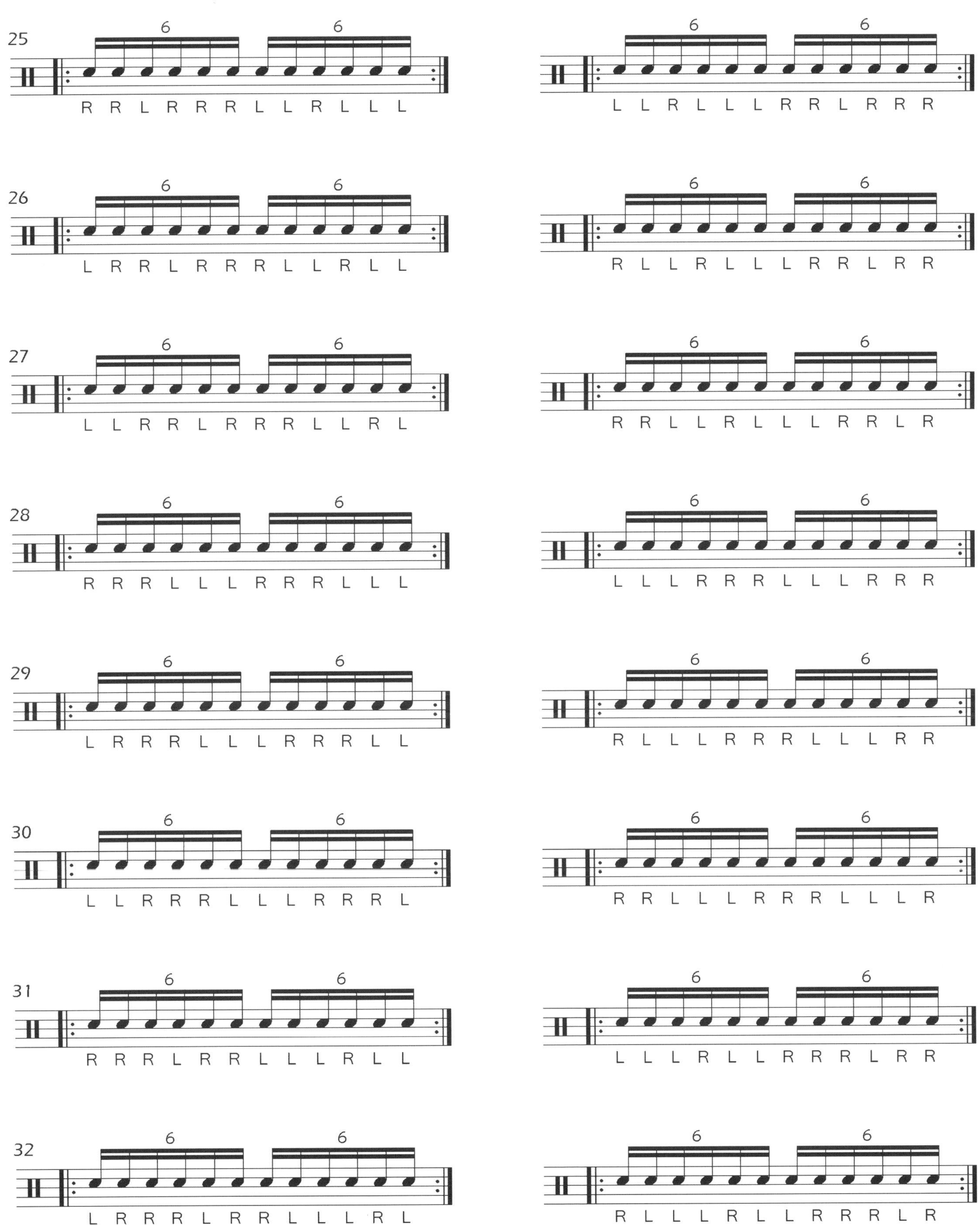

6-Note Combinations

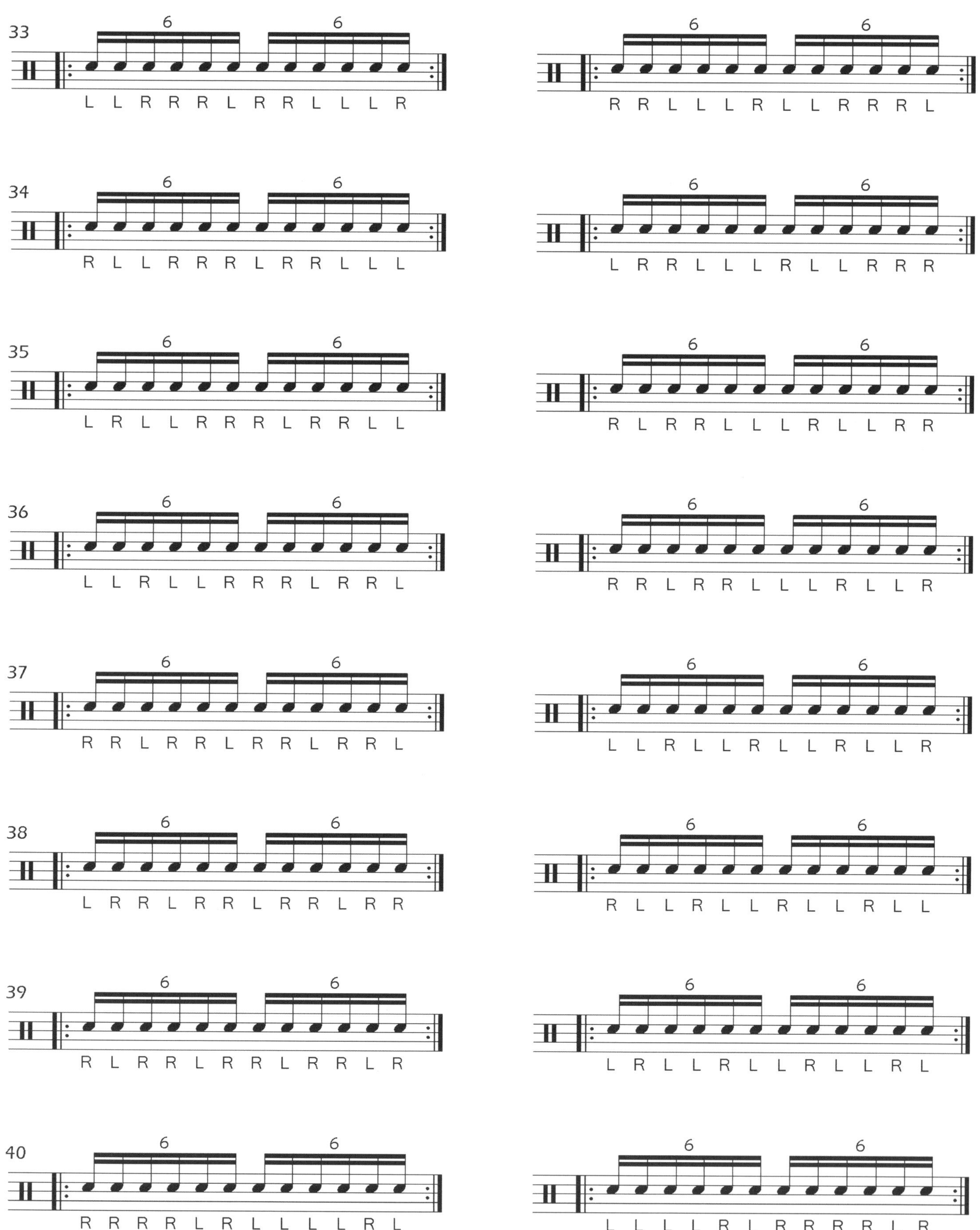

6-Note Combinations

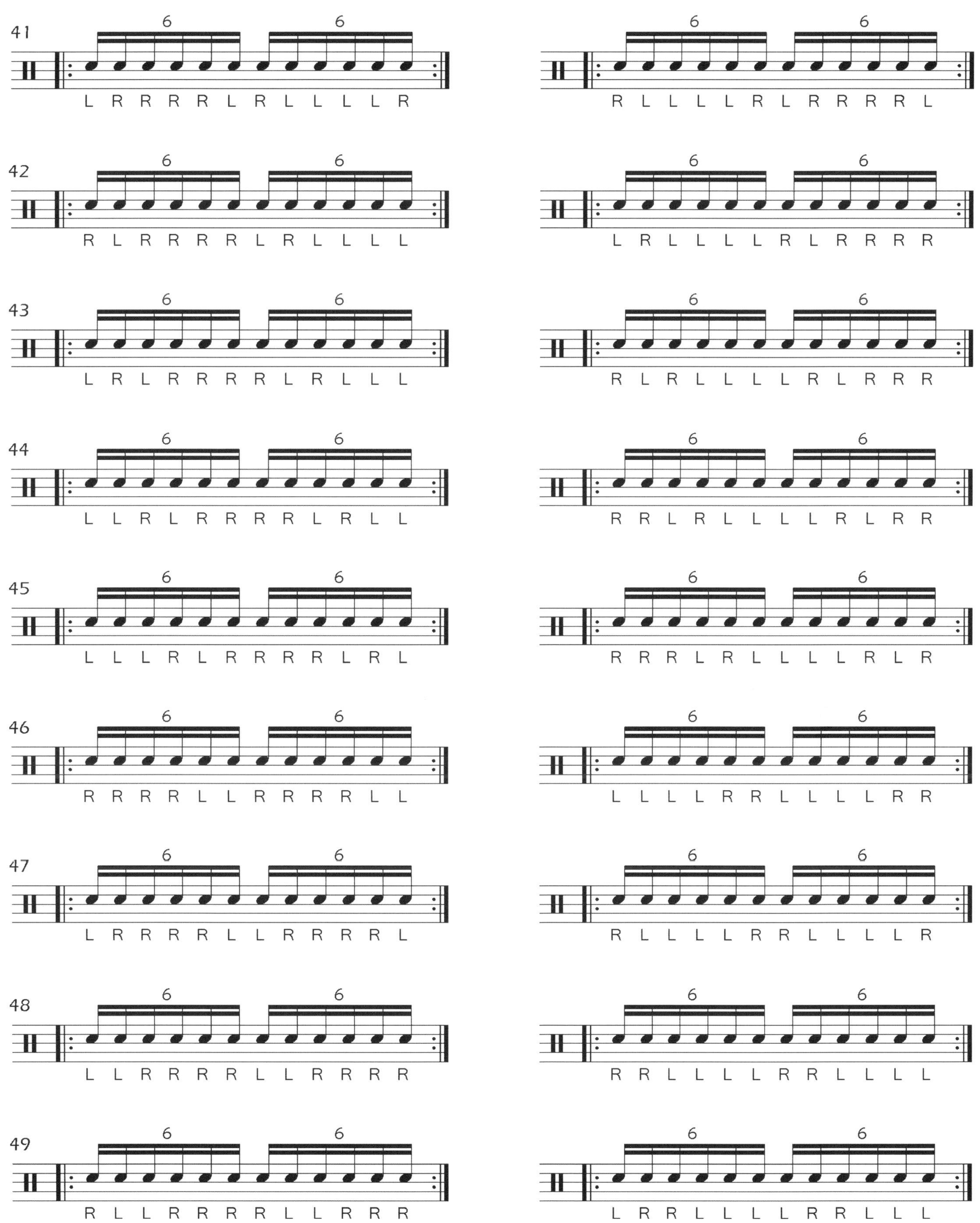

6-Note Combinations

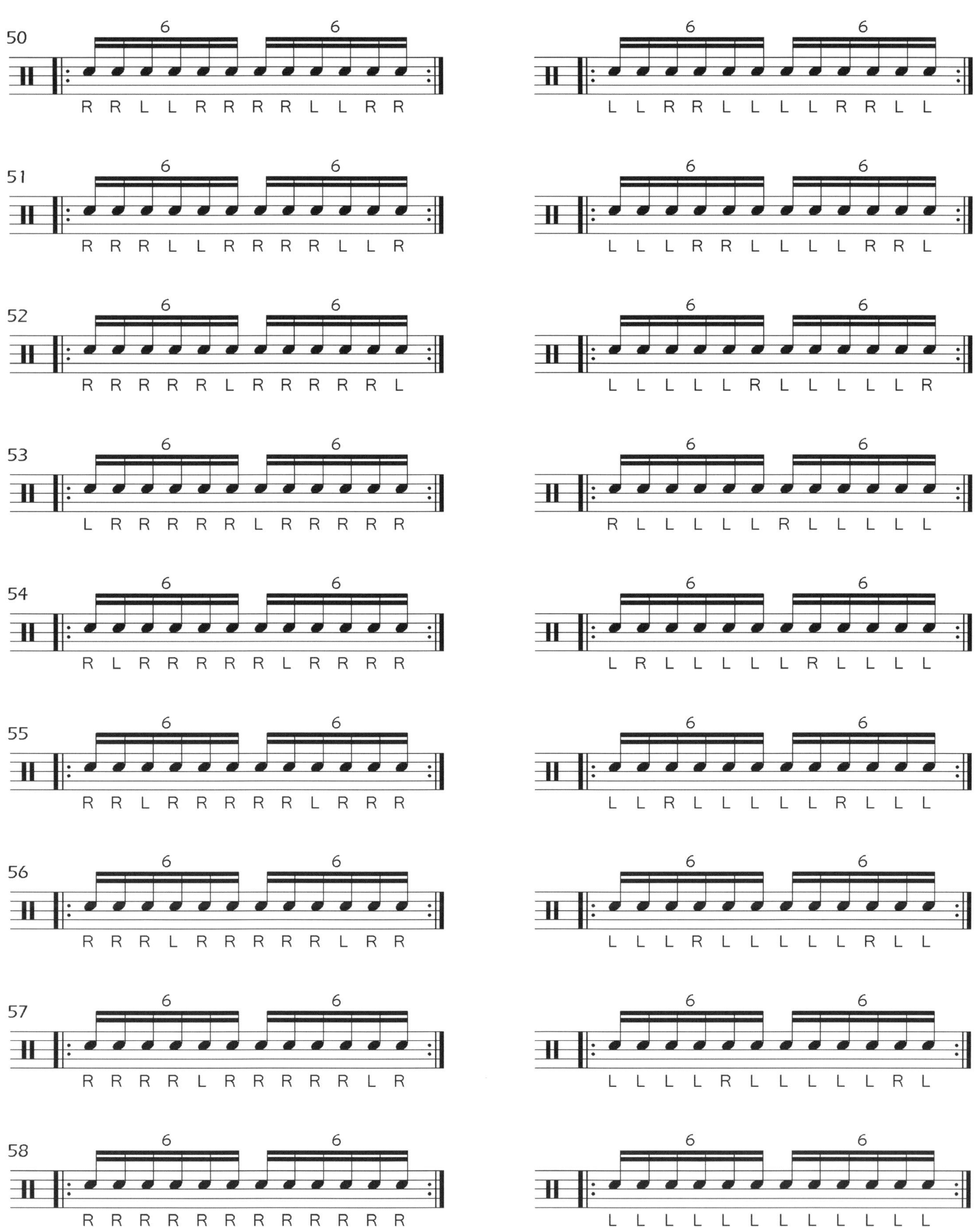

6-Note Combinations

- RHYTHM CHART -

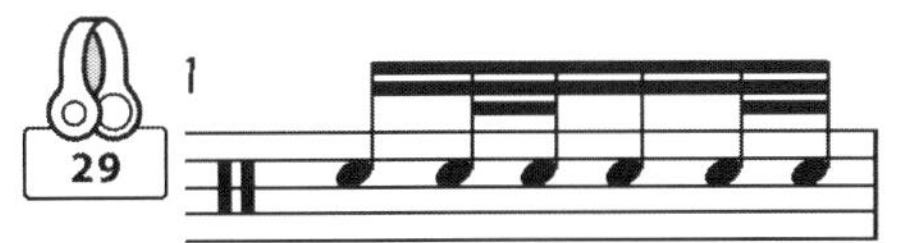

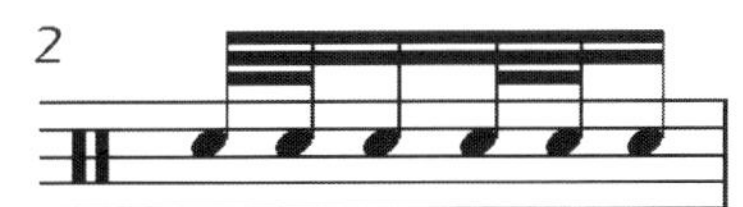

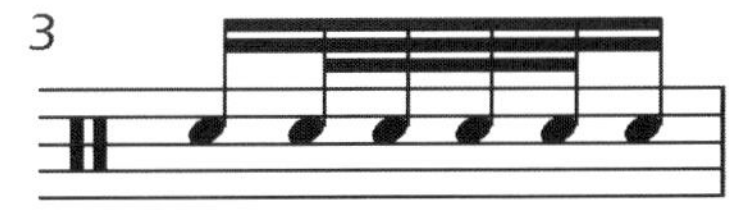

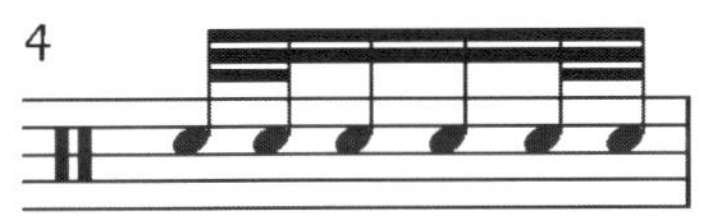

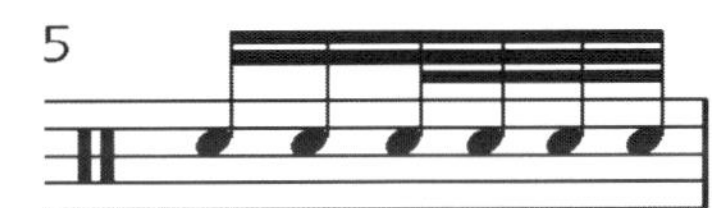

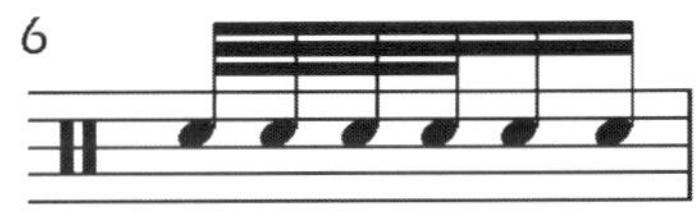

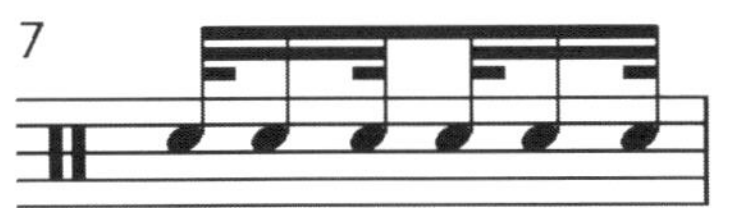

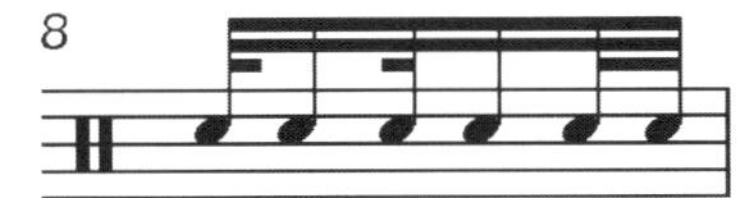

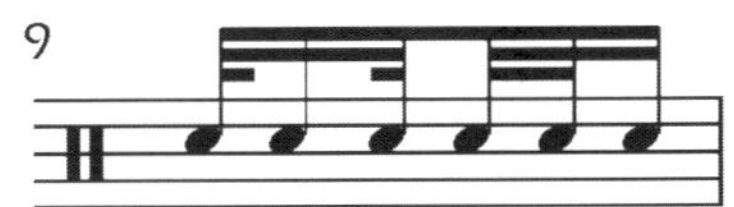

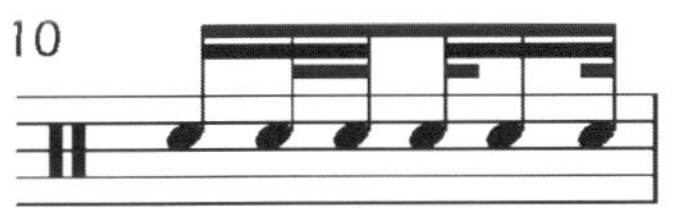

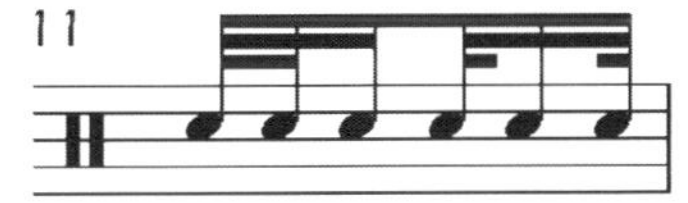

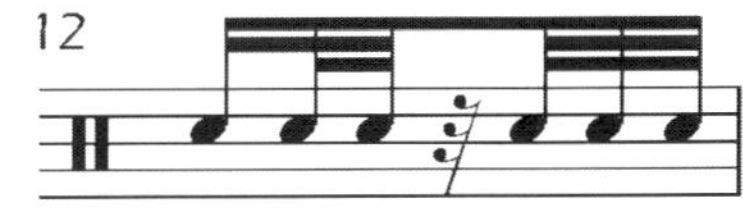

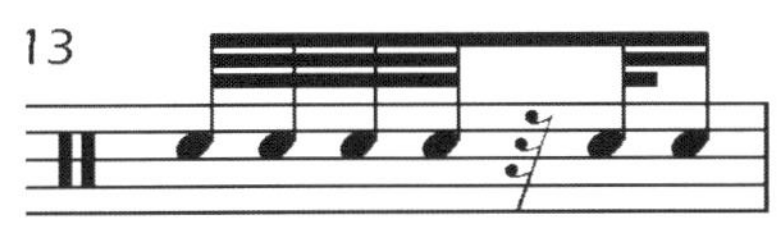

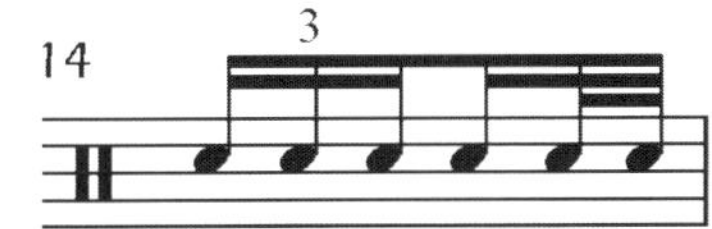

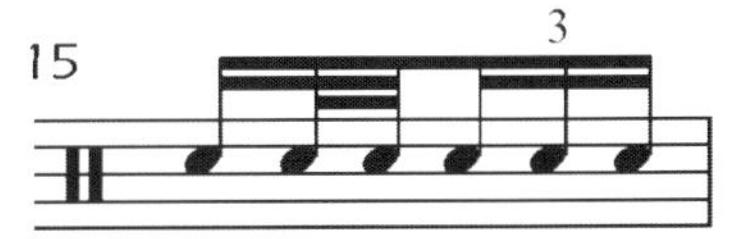

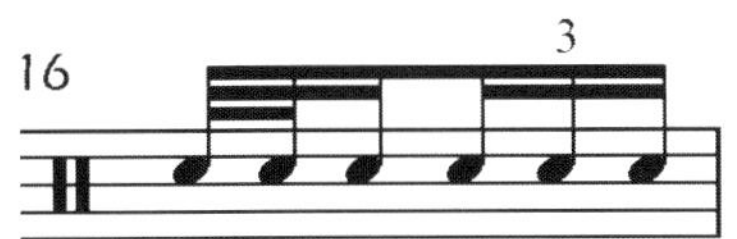

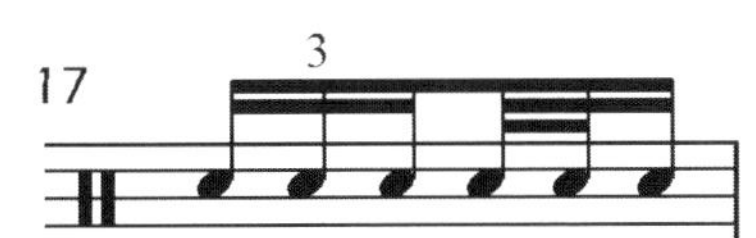

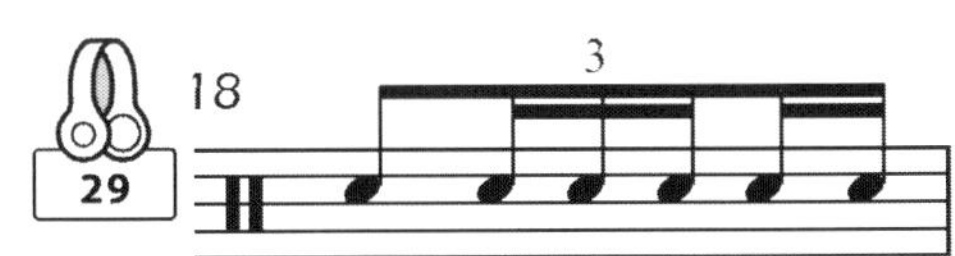

7-Note Combinations

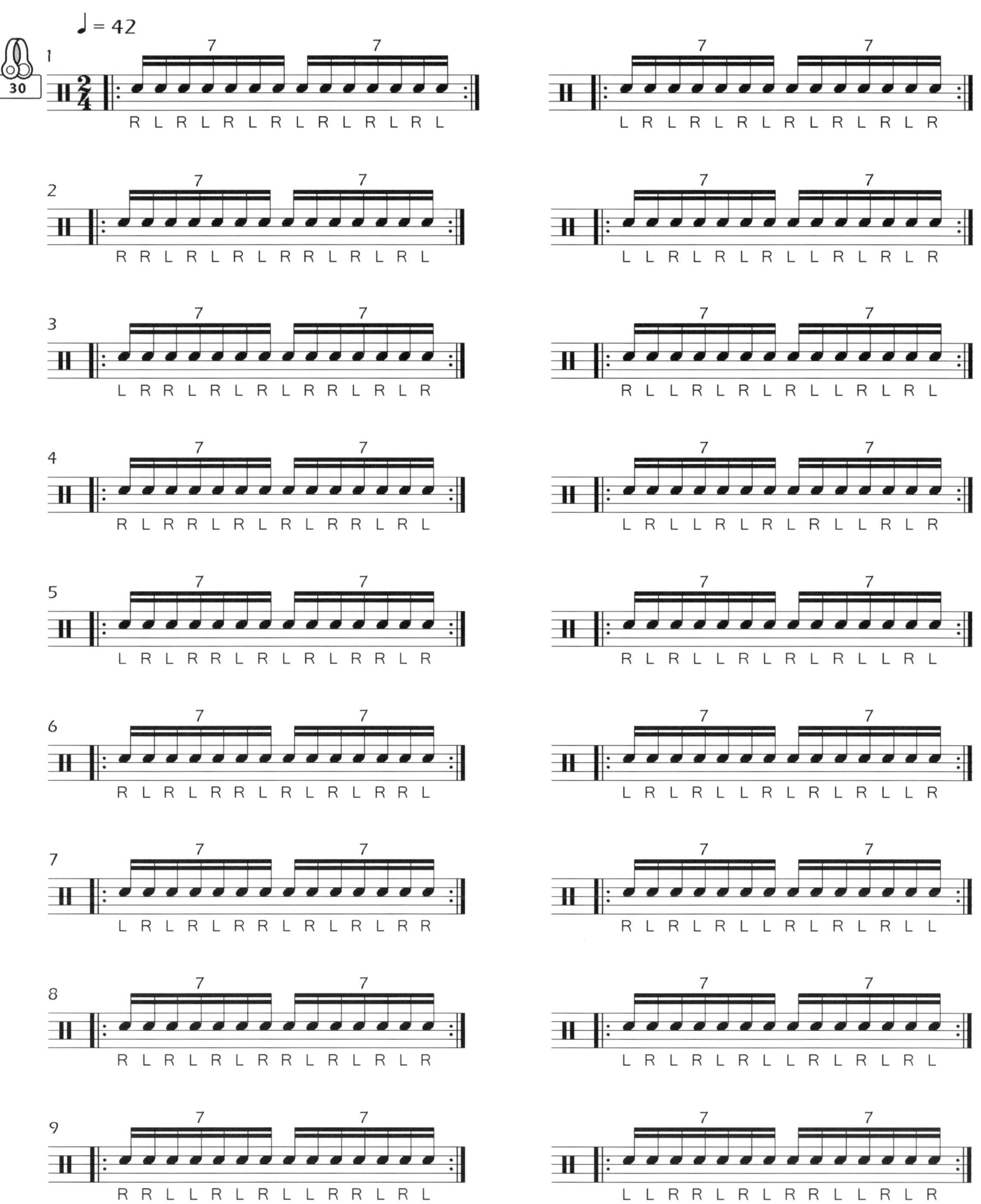

7-Note Combinations

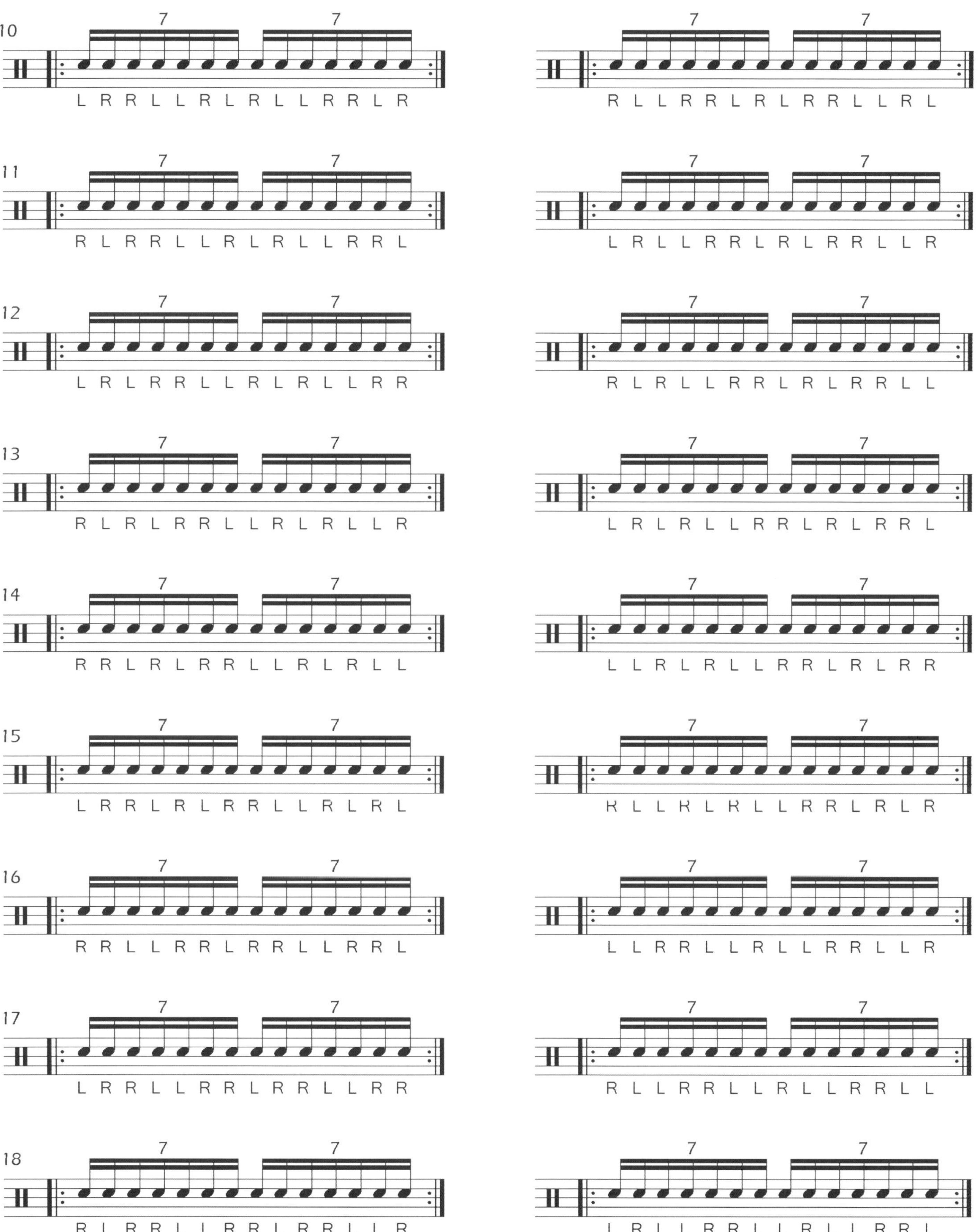

7-Note Combinations

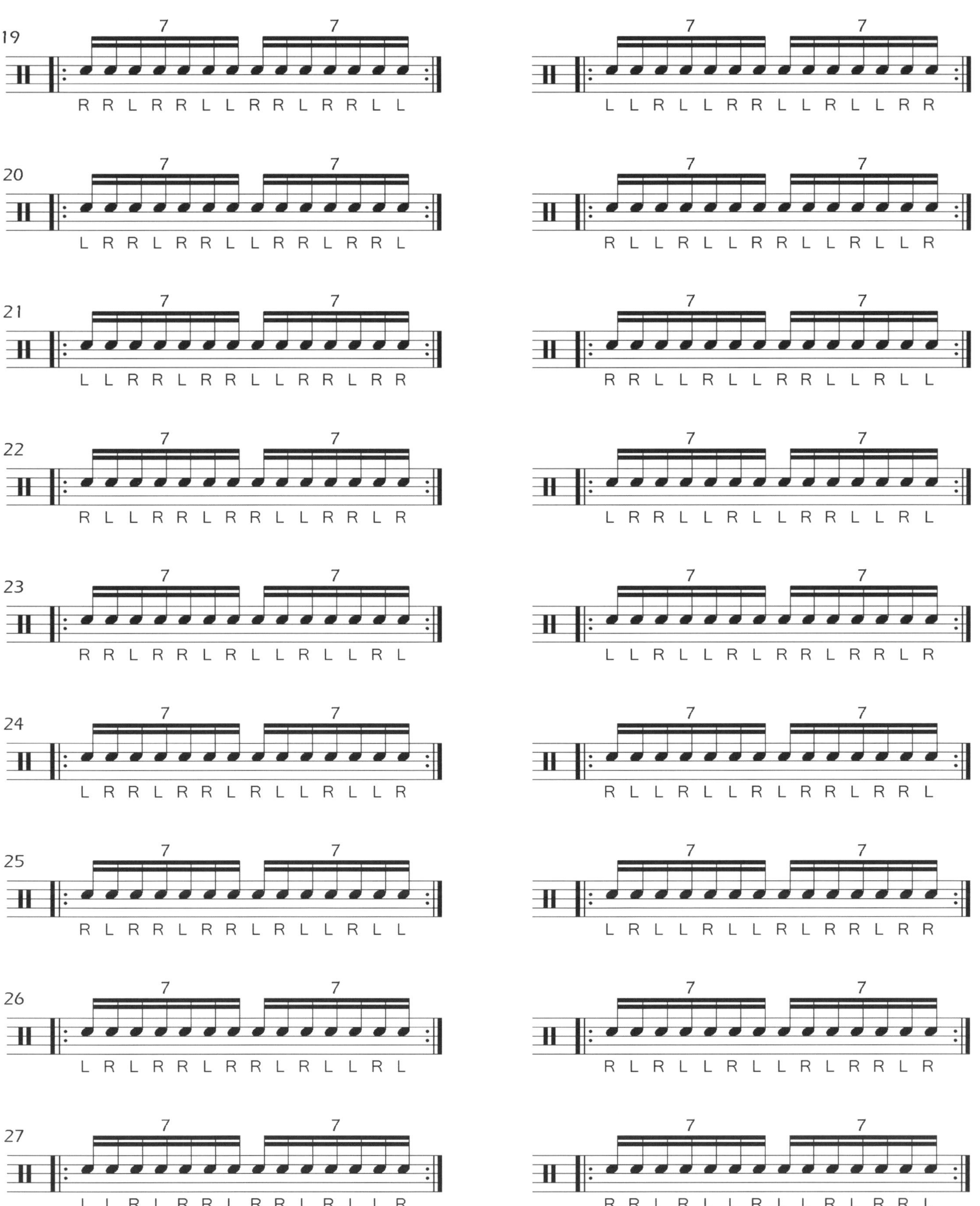

7-Note Combinations

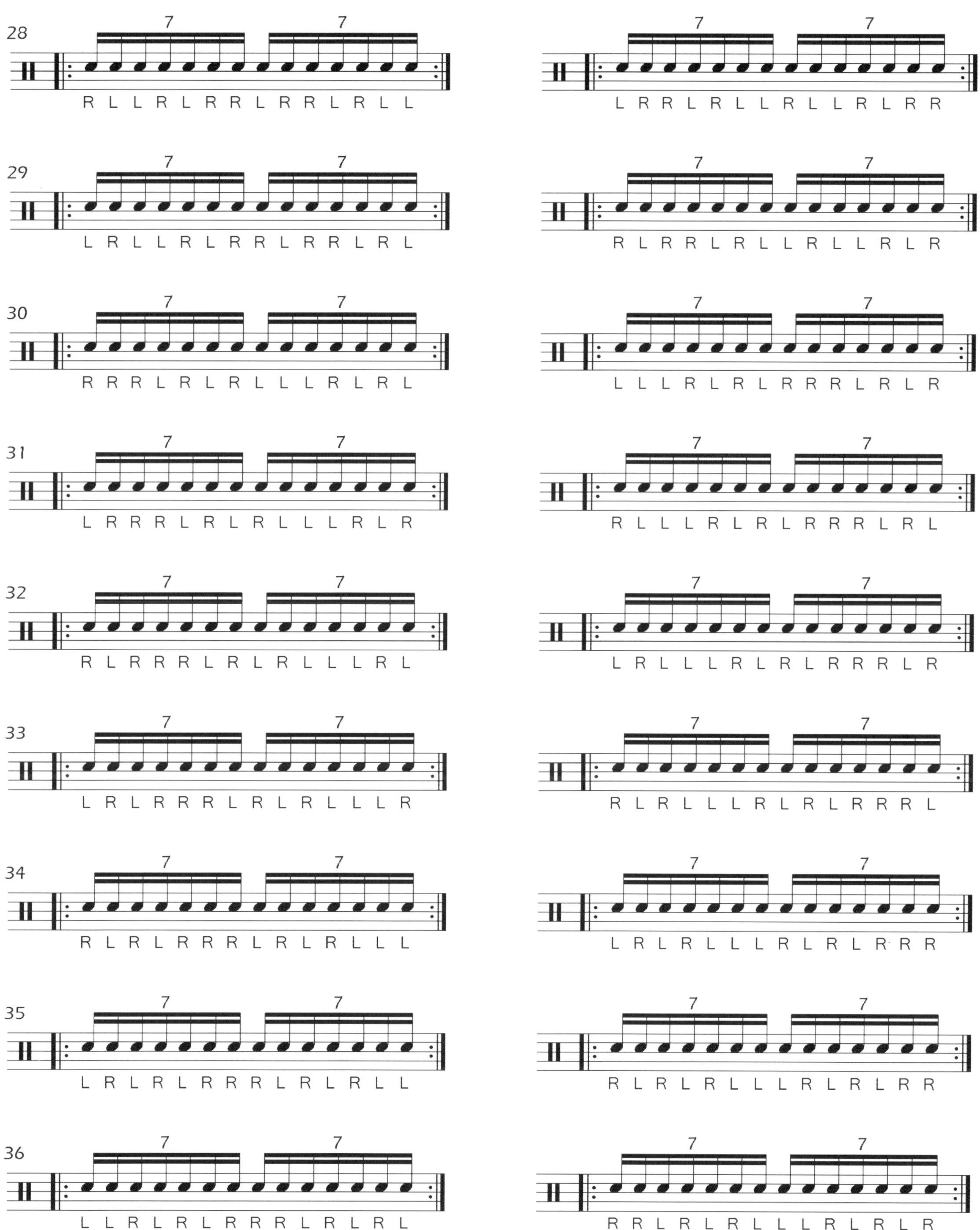

7-Note Combinations

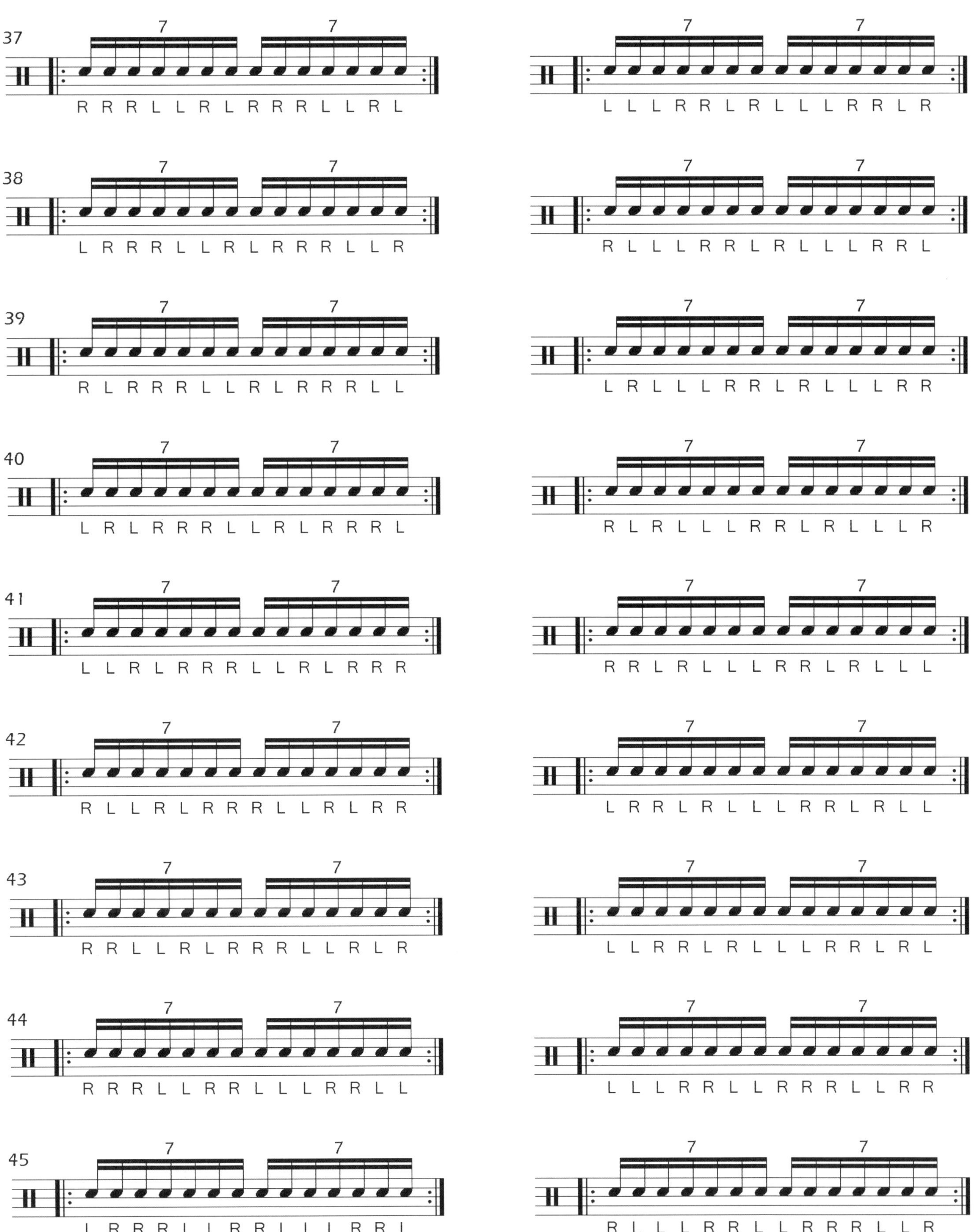

7-Note Combinations

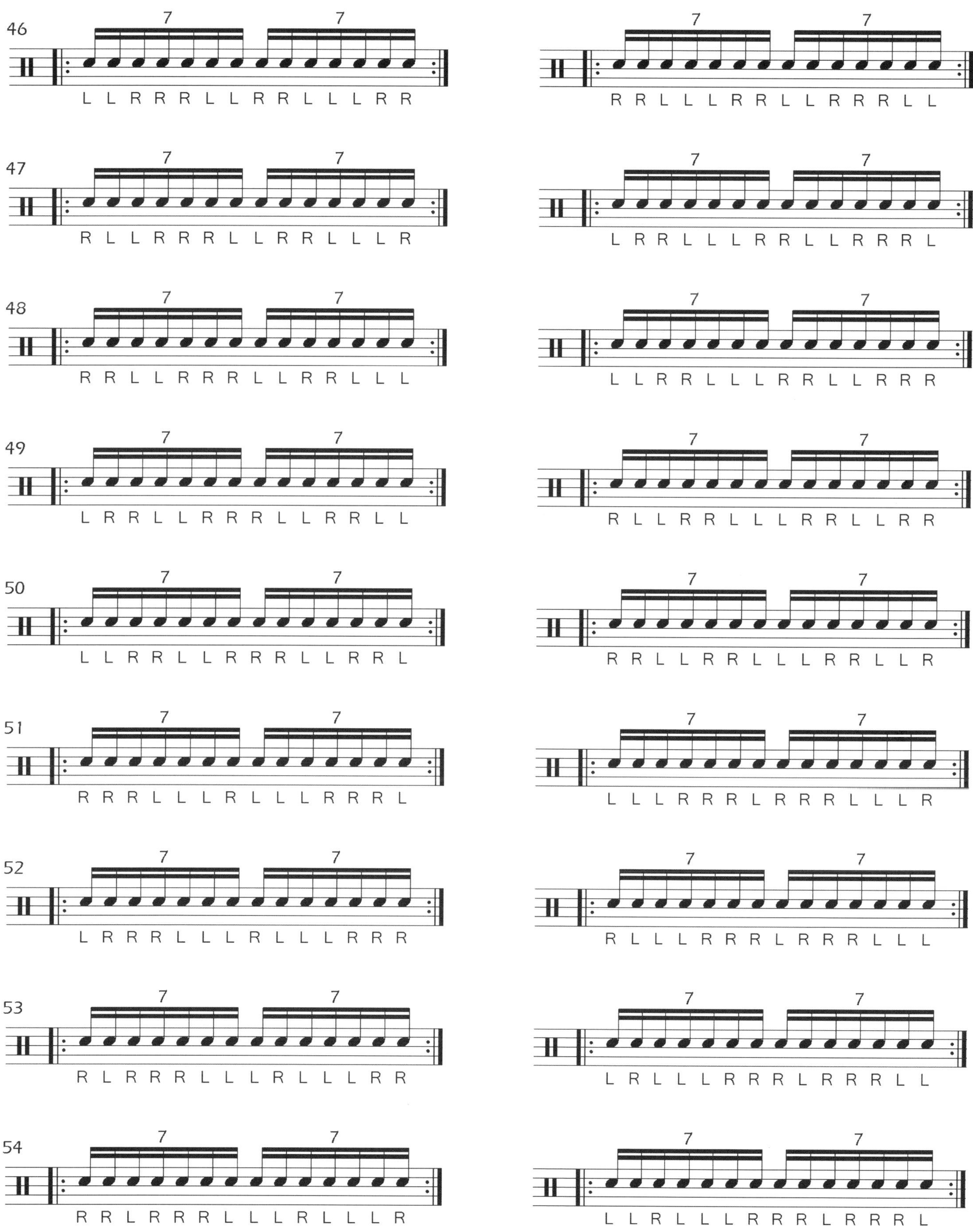

7-Note Combinations

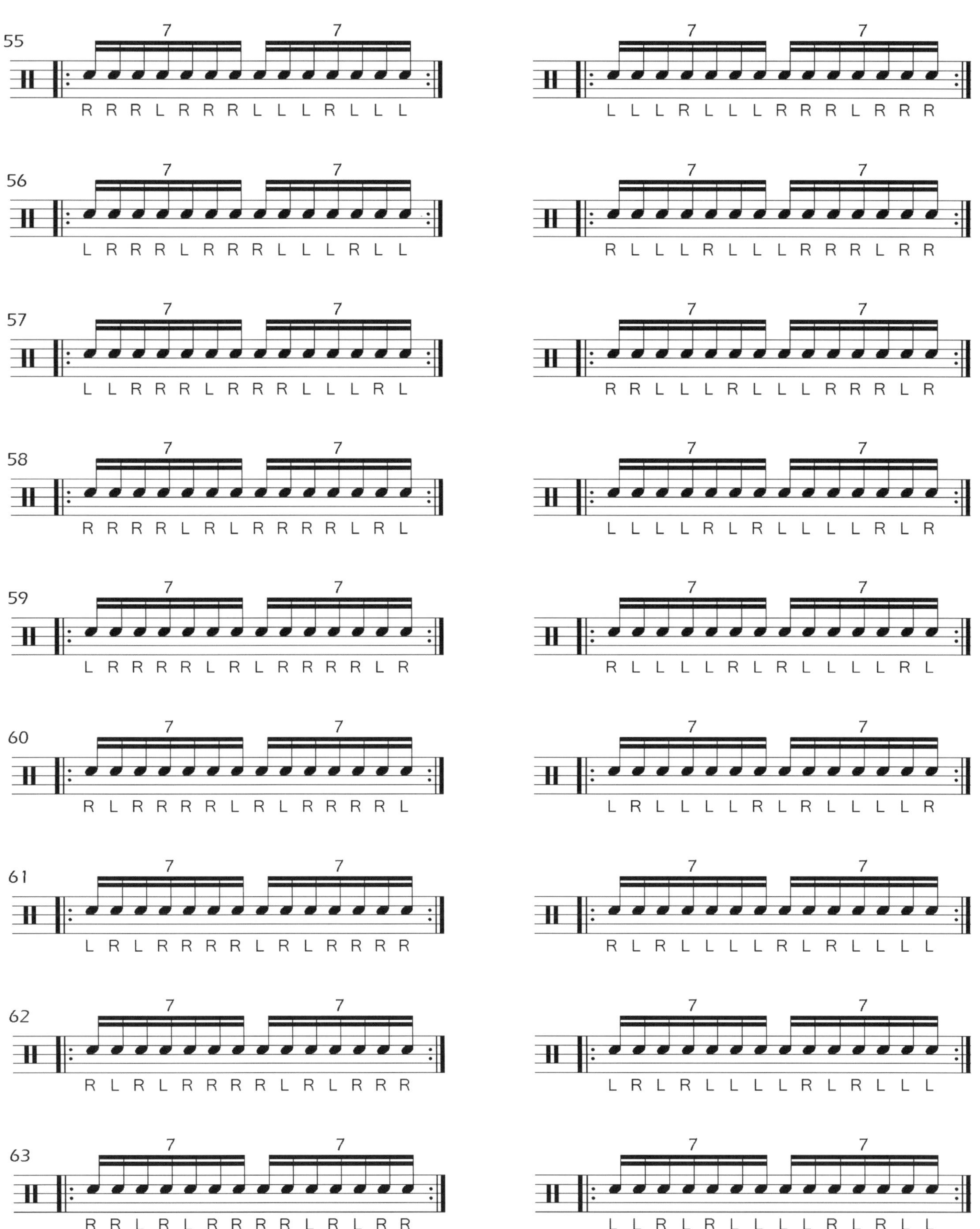

7-Note Combinations

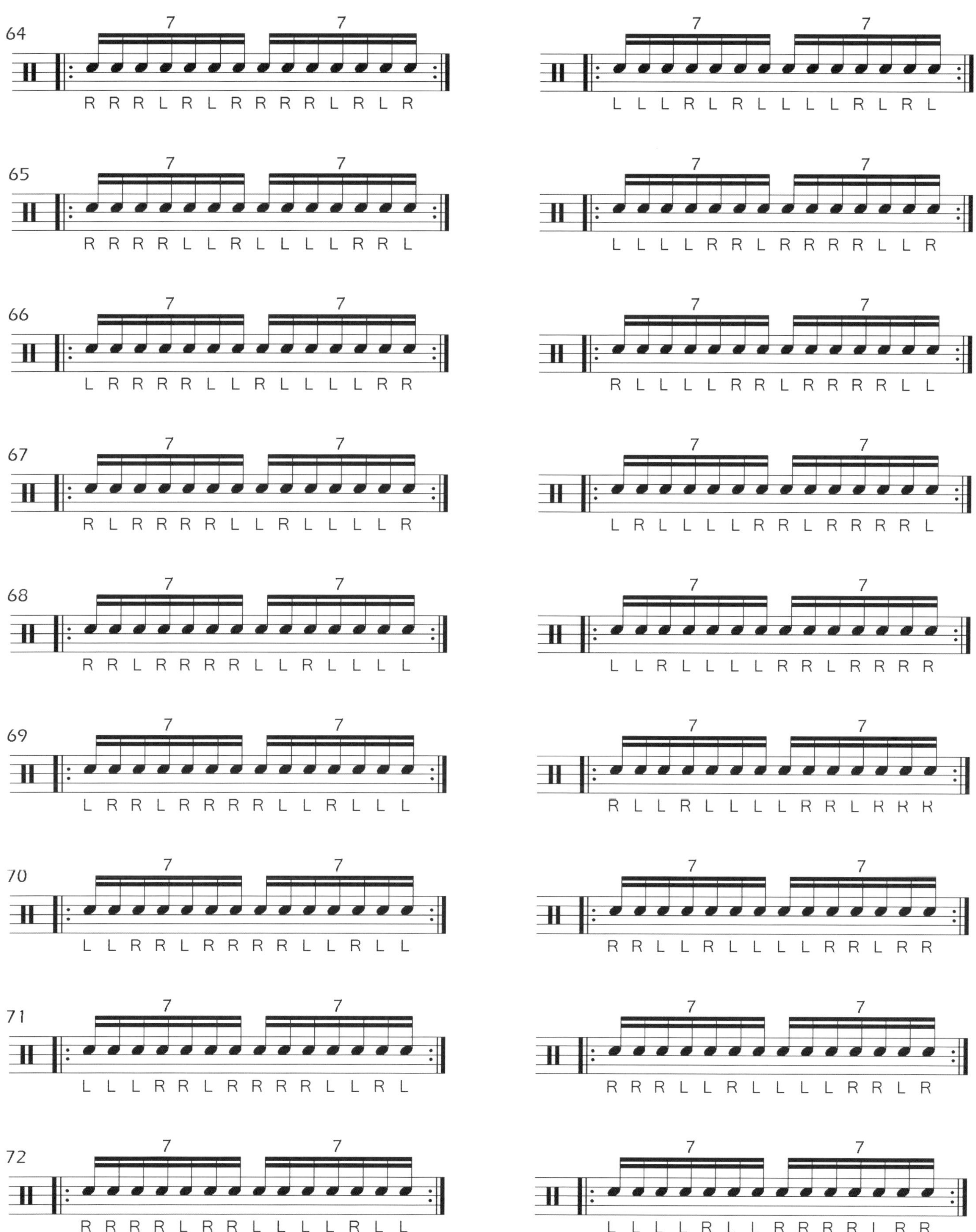

7-Note Combinations

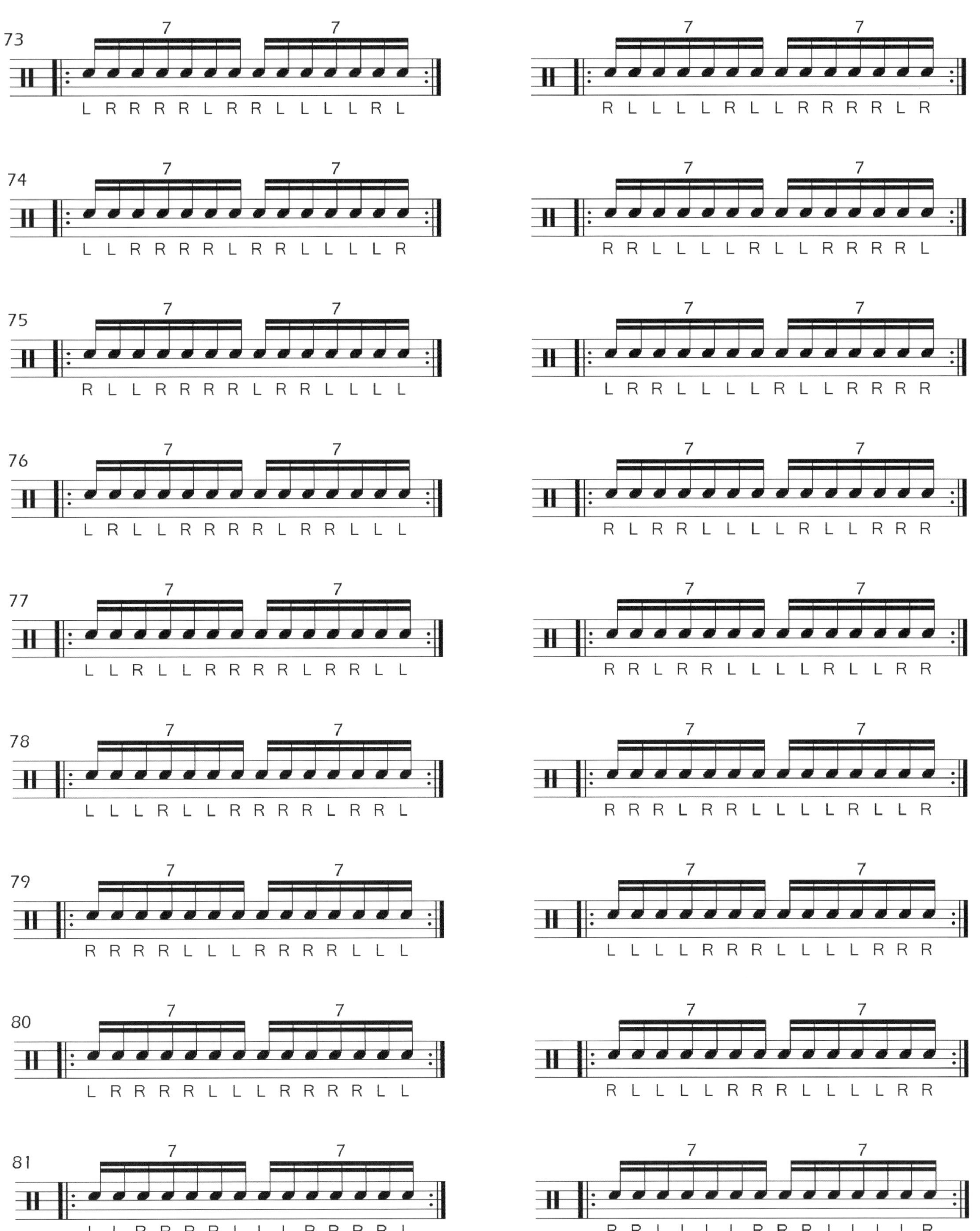

7-Note Combinations

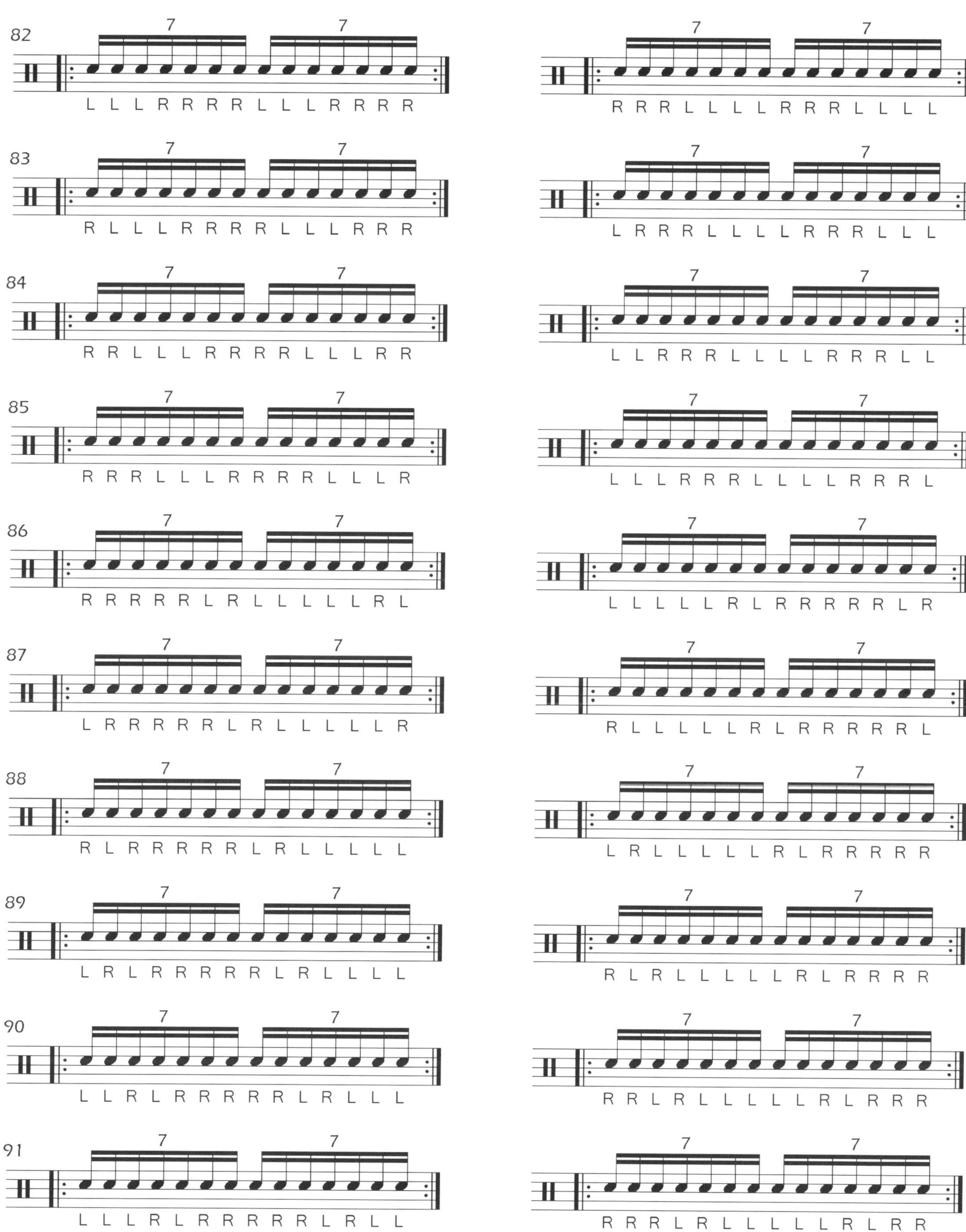

7-Note Combinations

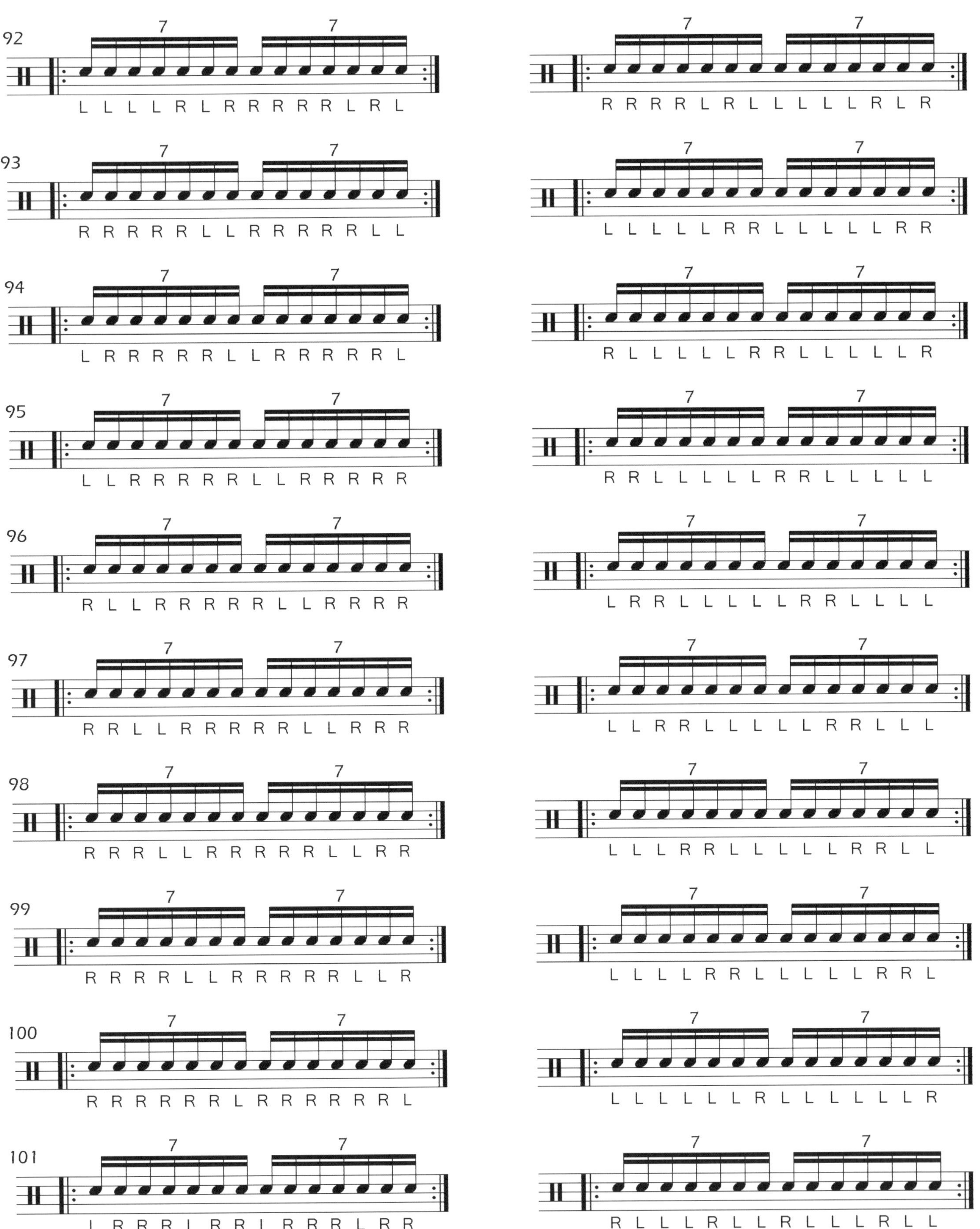

7-Note Combinations

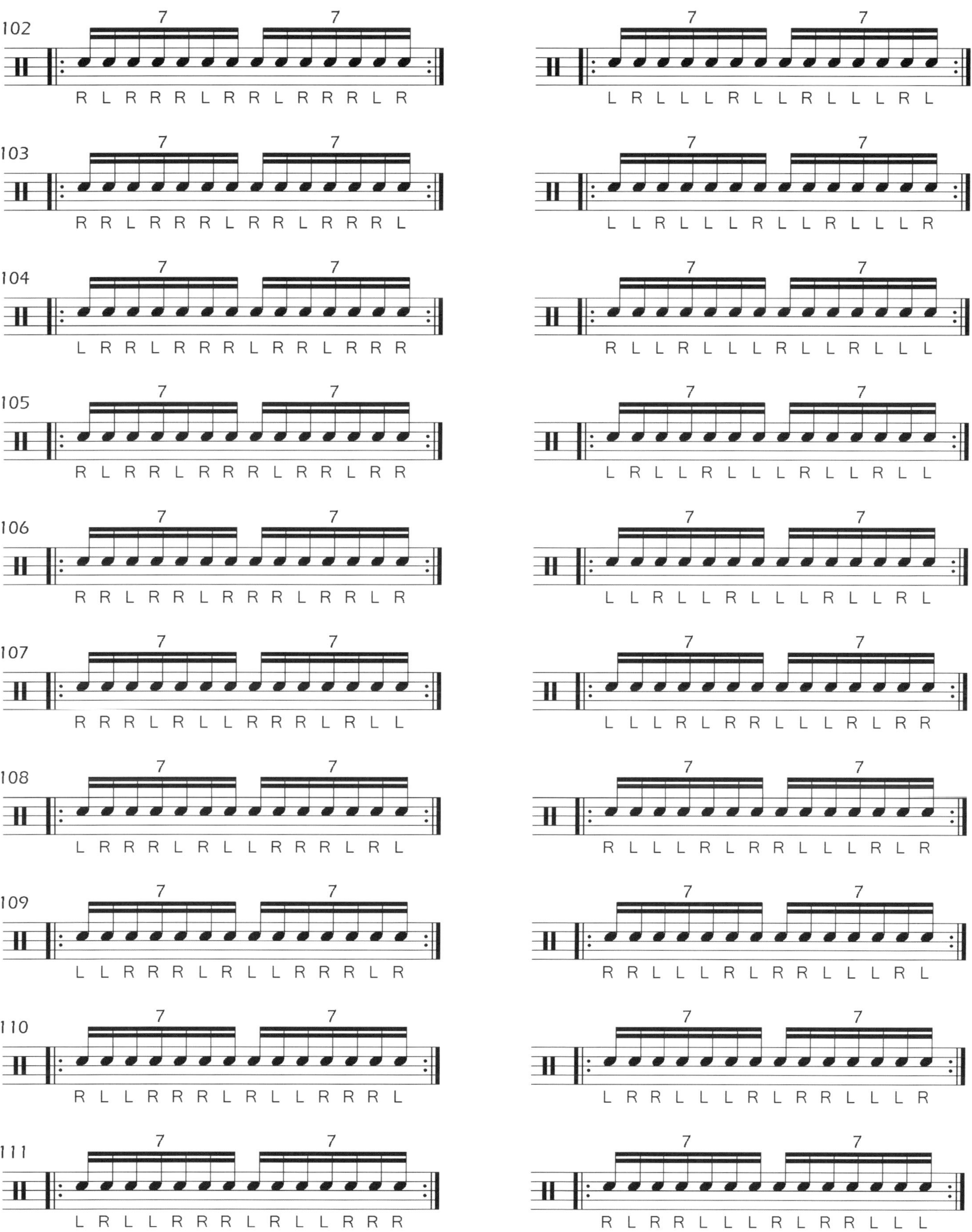

7-Note Combinations

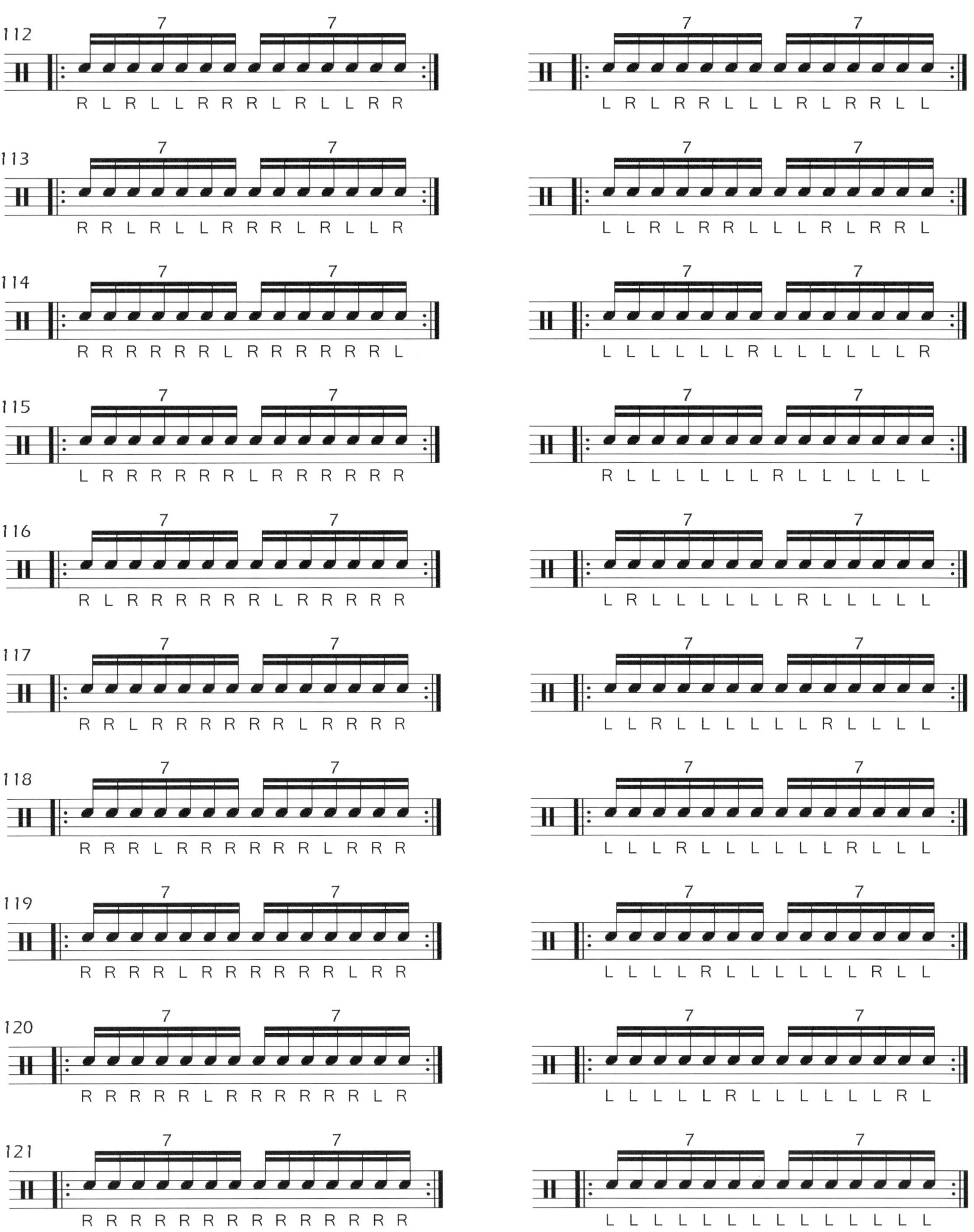

7-Note Combinations

- RHYTHM CHART -

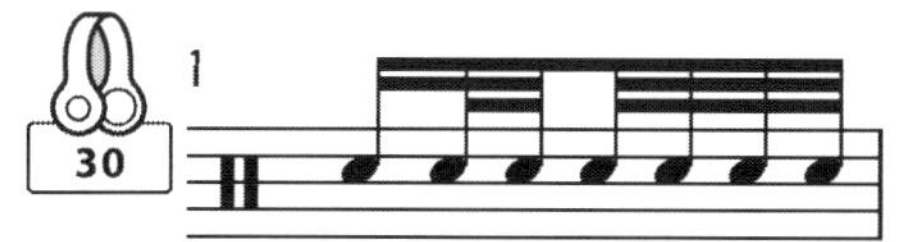

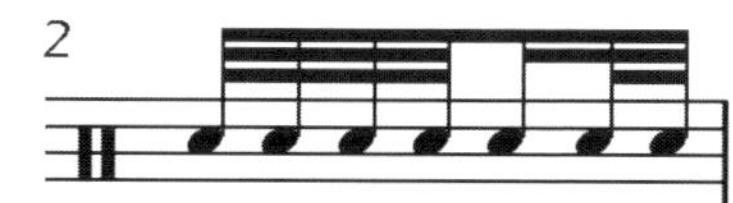

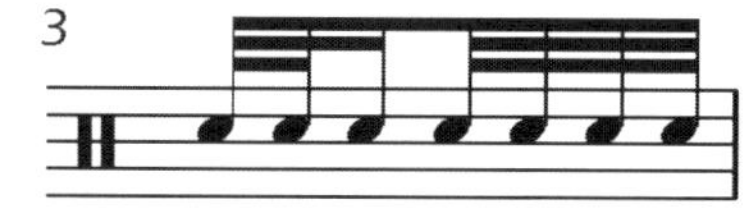

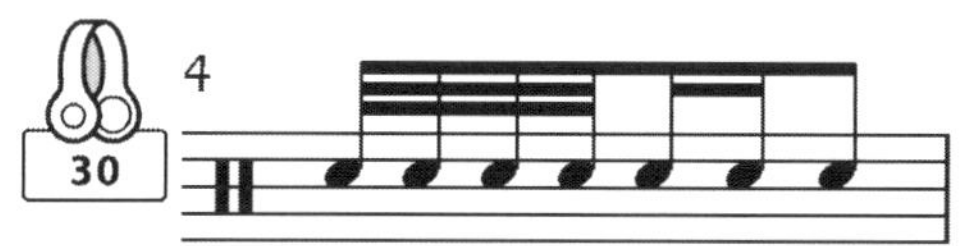

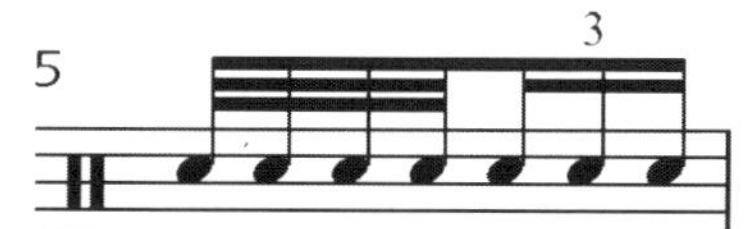

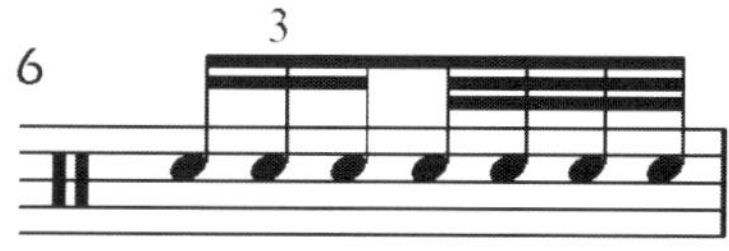

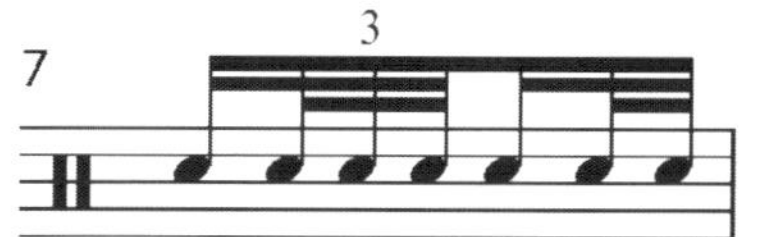

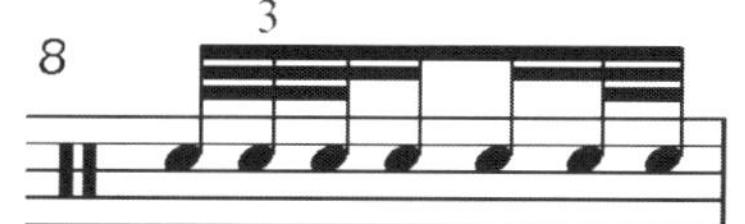

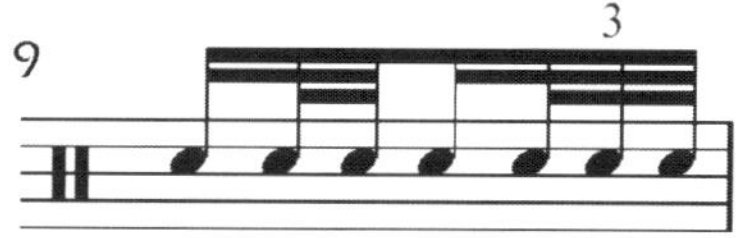

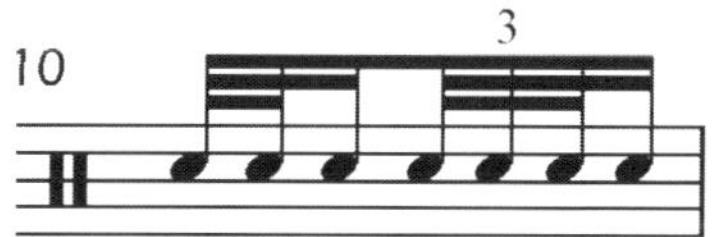

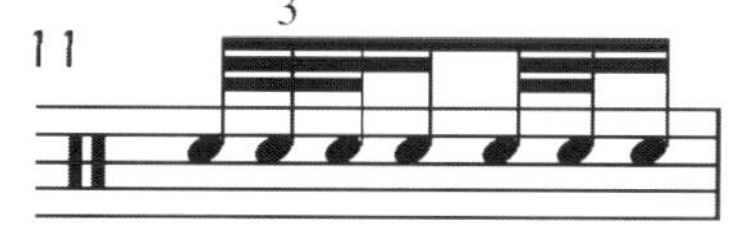

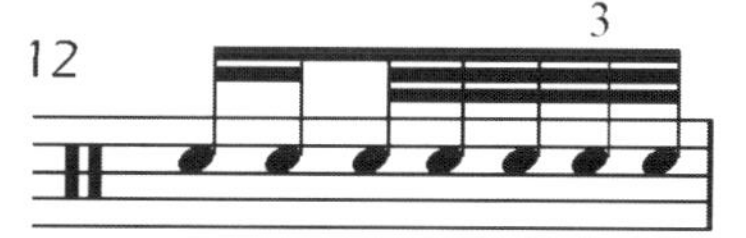

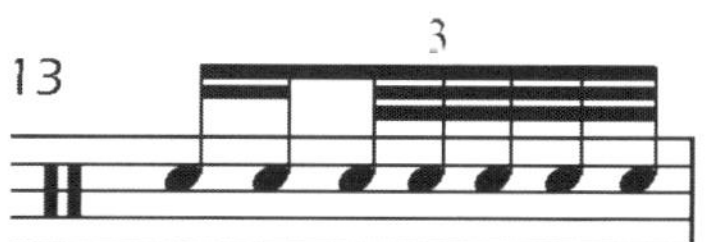

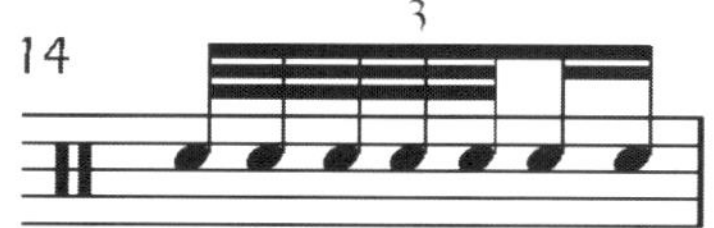

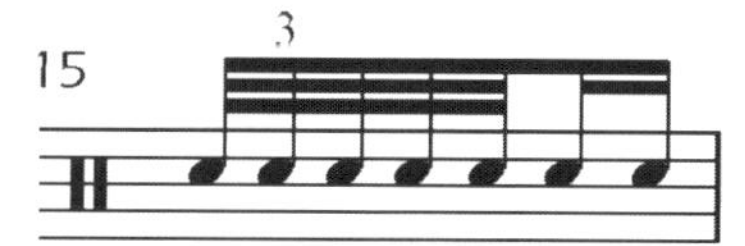

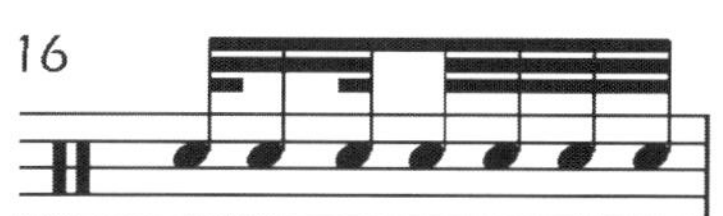

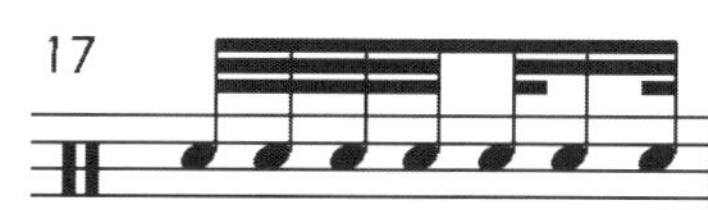

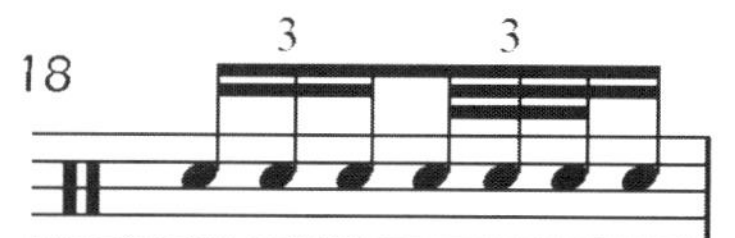

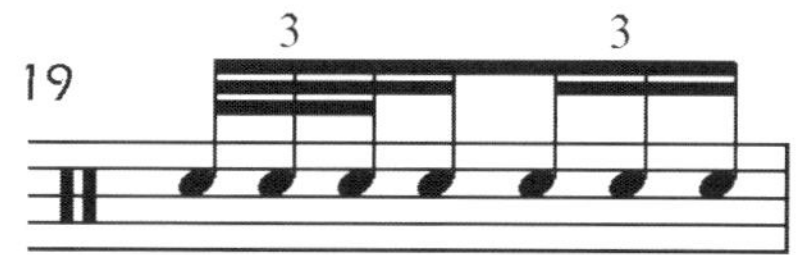

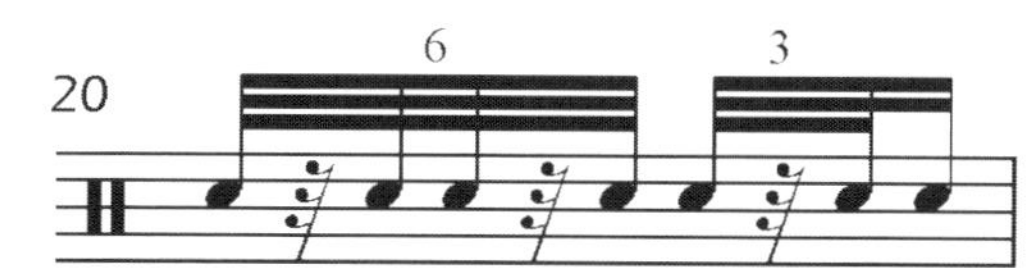

8-Note Combinations

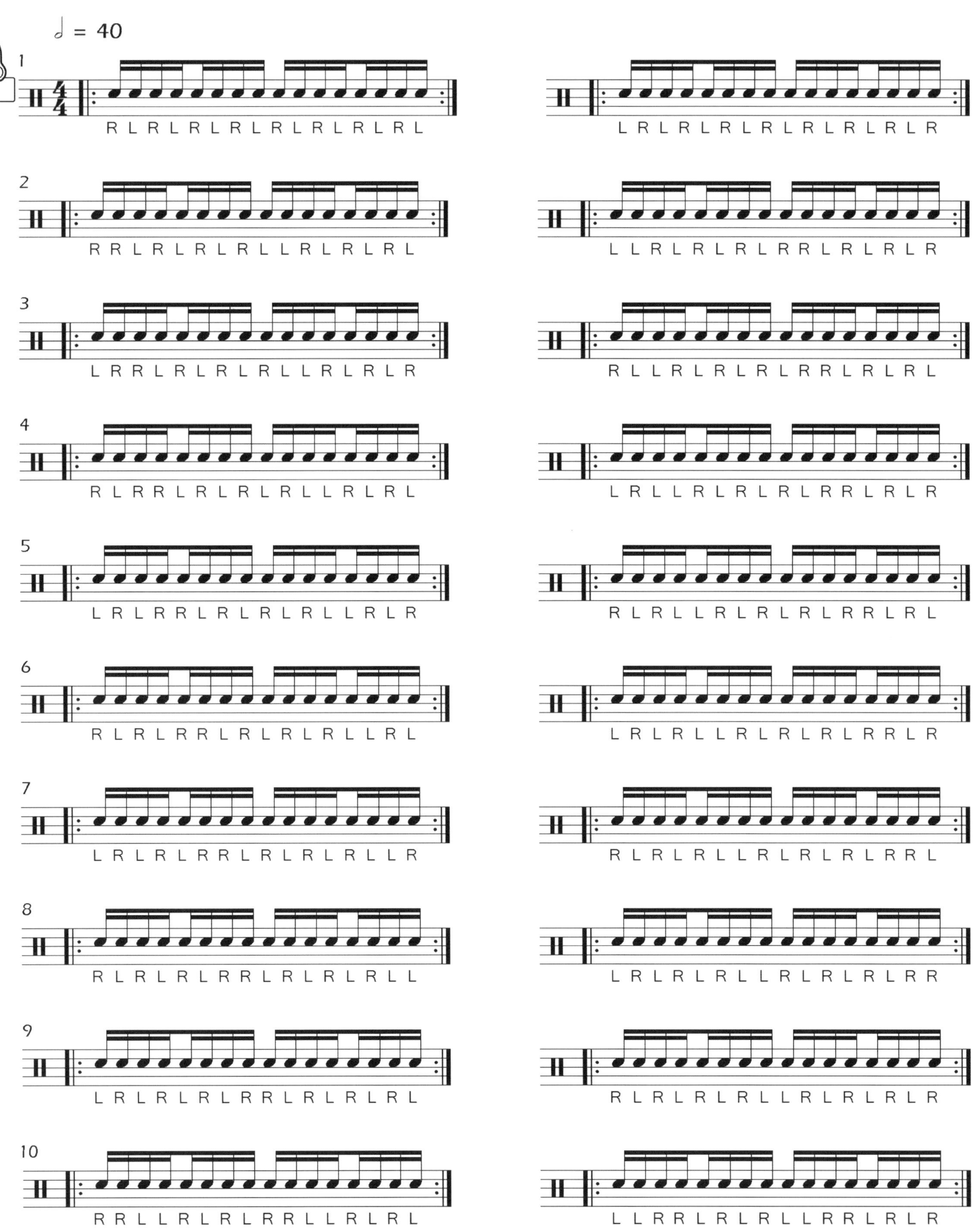

8-Note Combinations

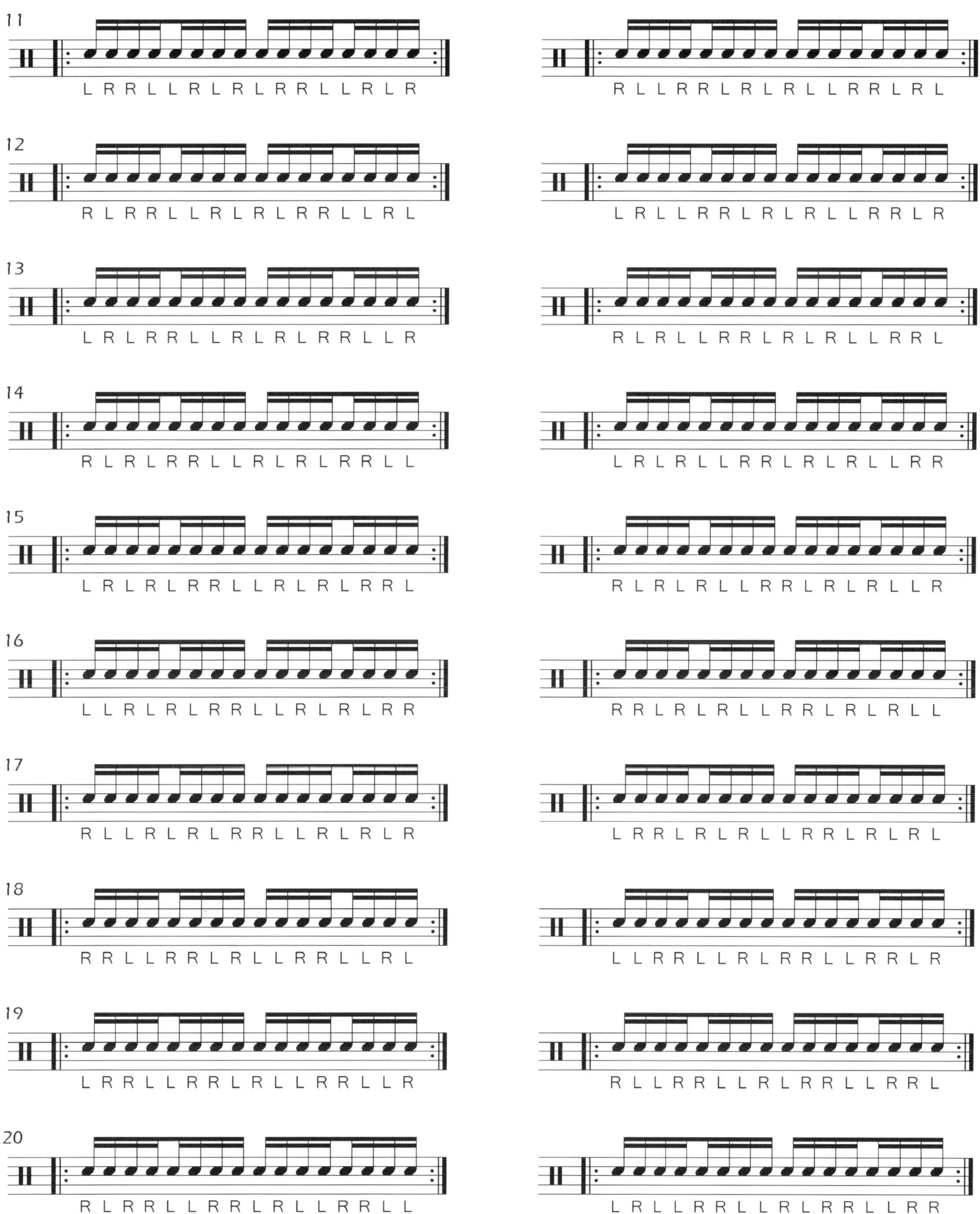

8-Note Combinations

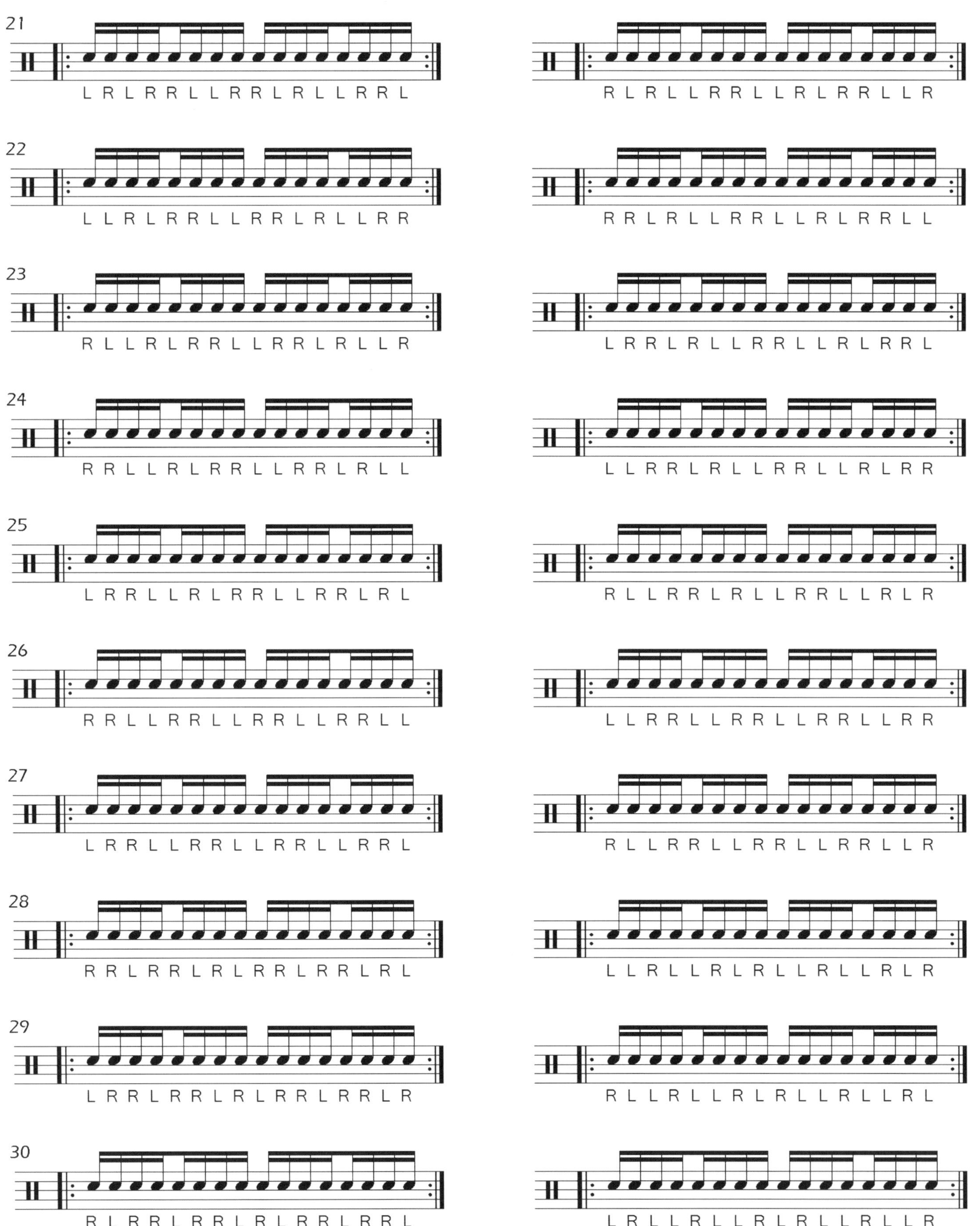

8-Note Combinations

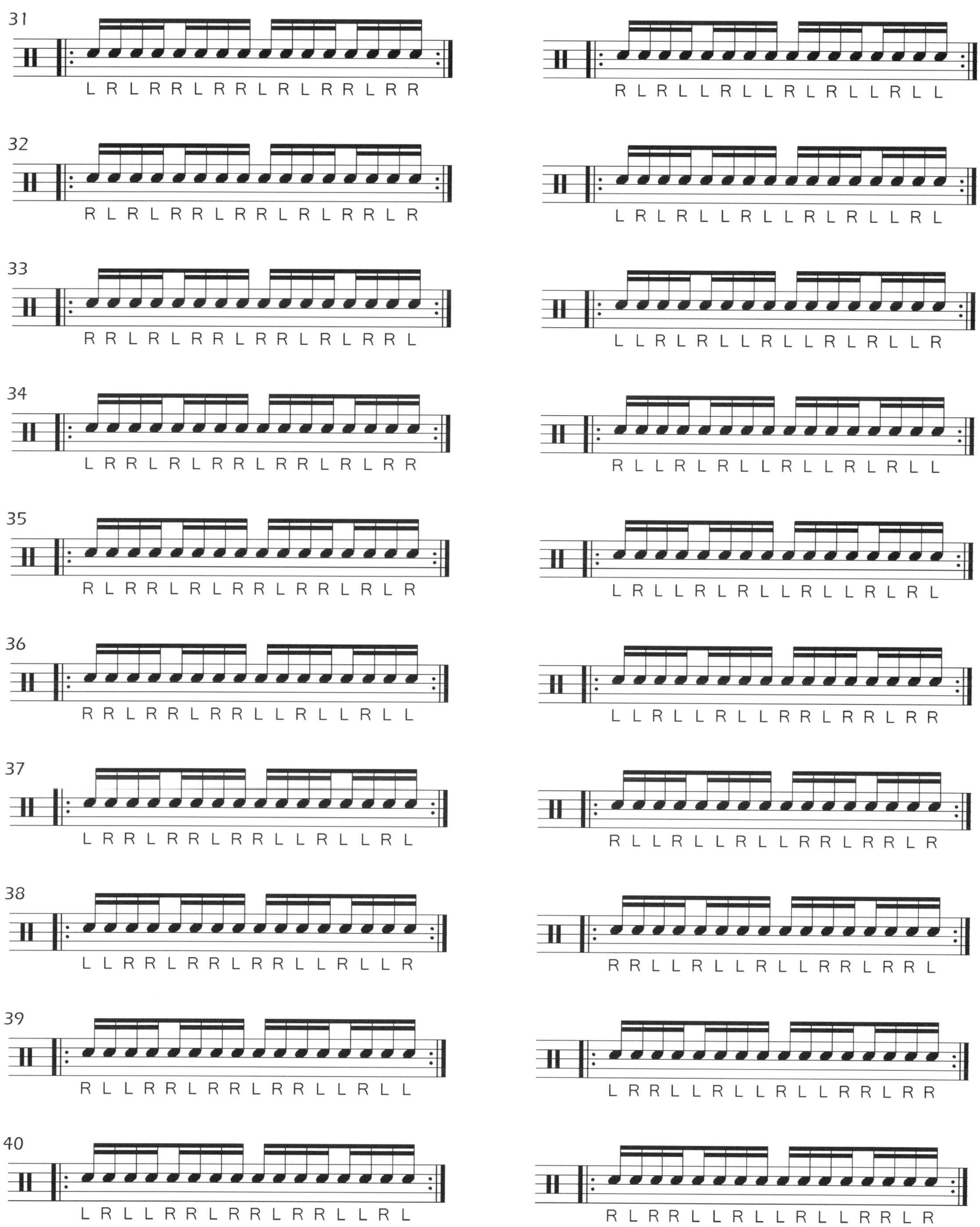

8-Note Combinations

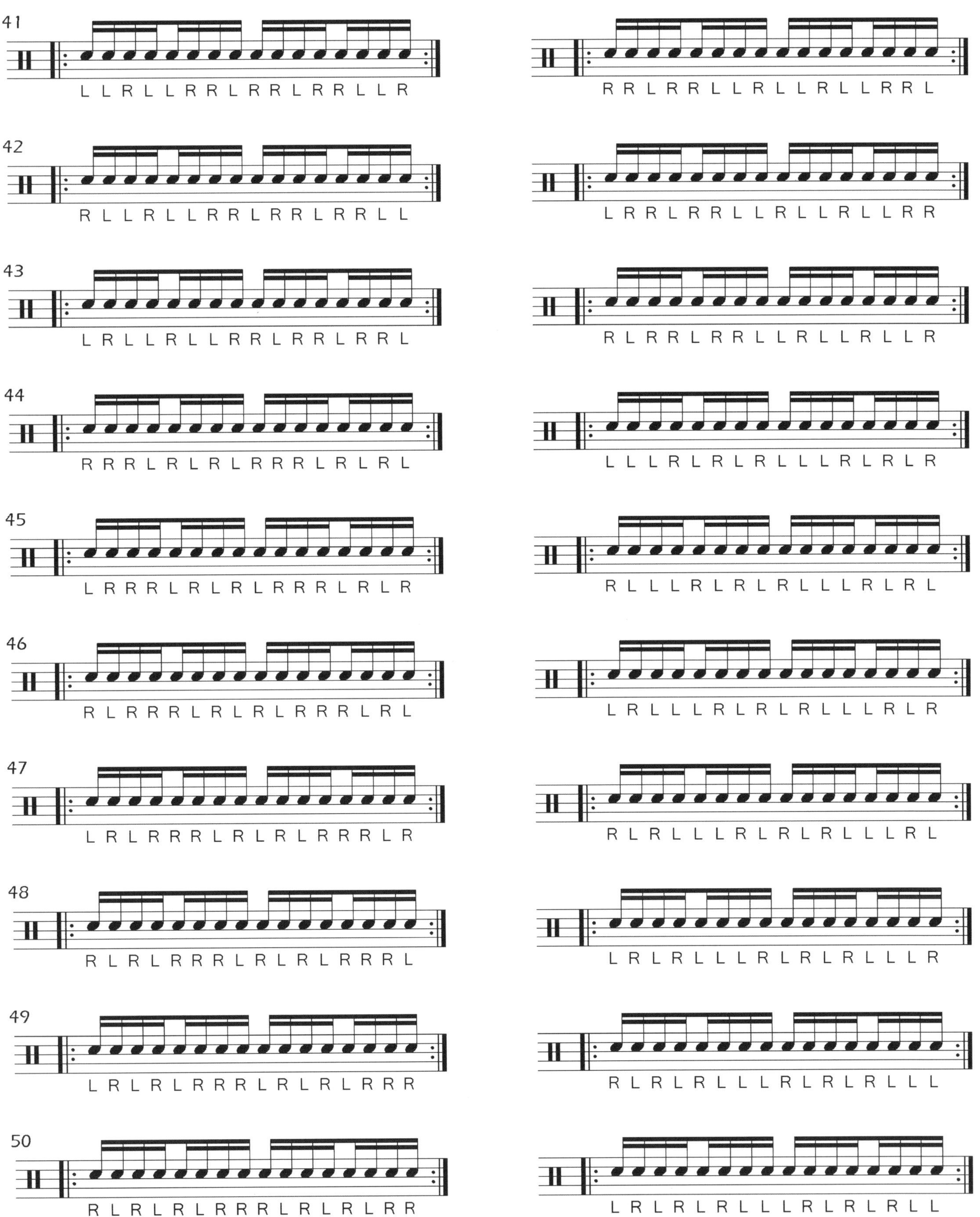

8-Note Combinations

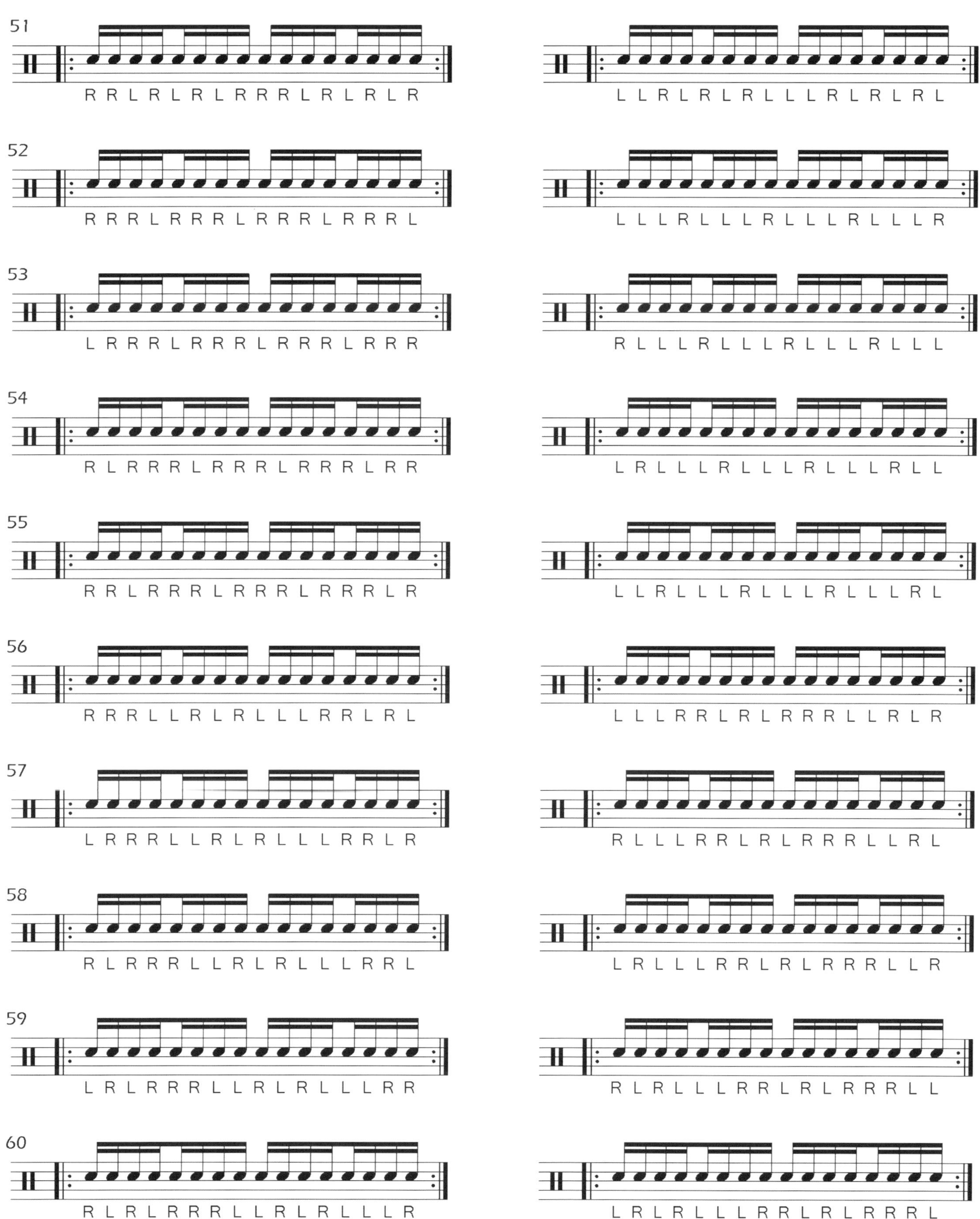

8-Note Combinations

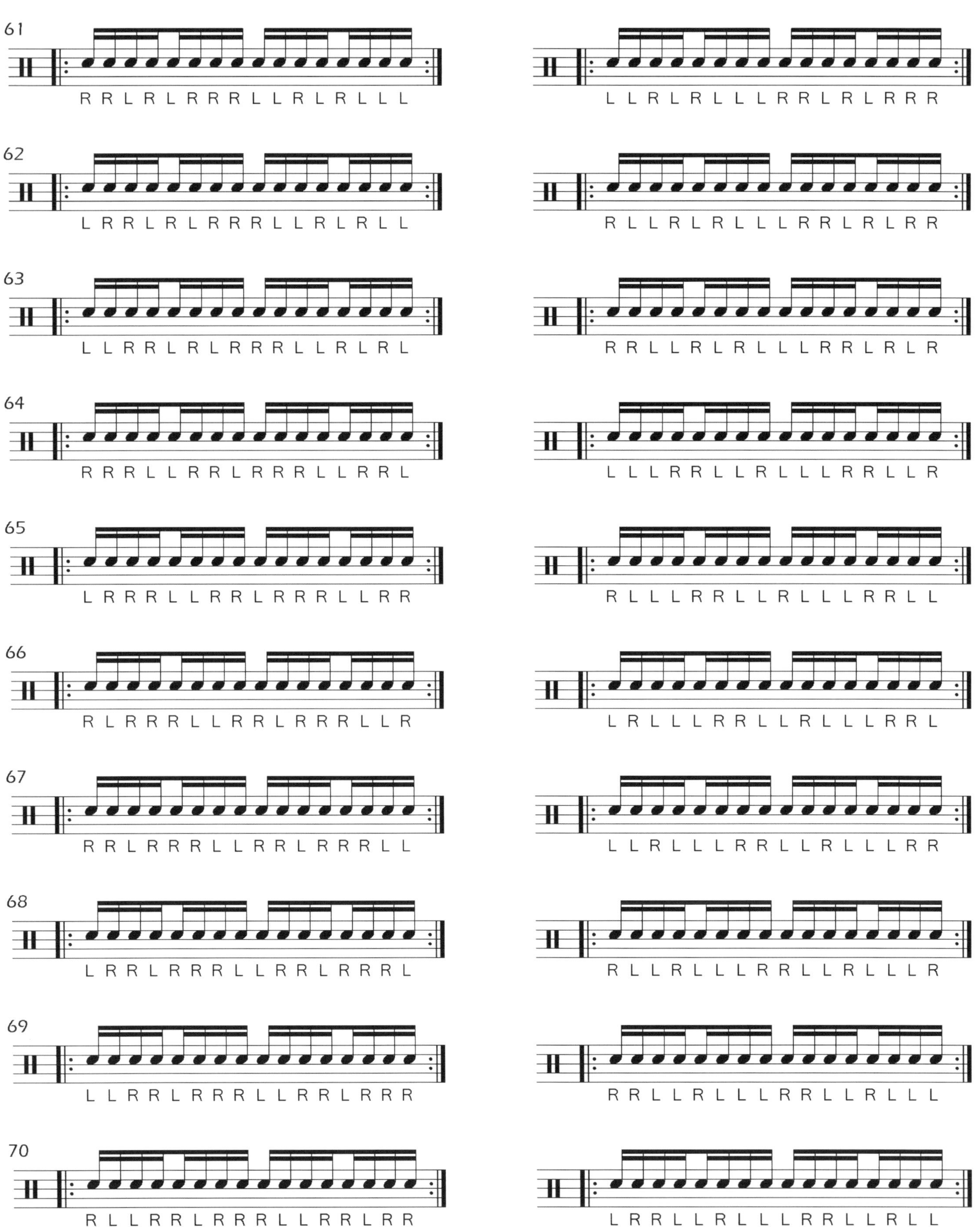

8-Note Combinations

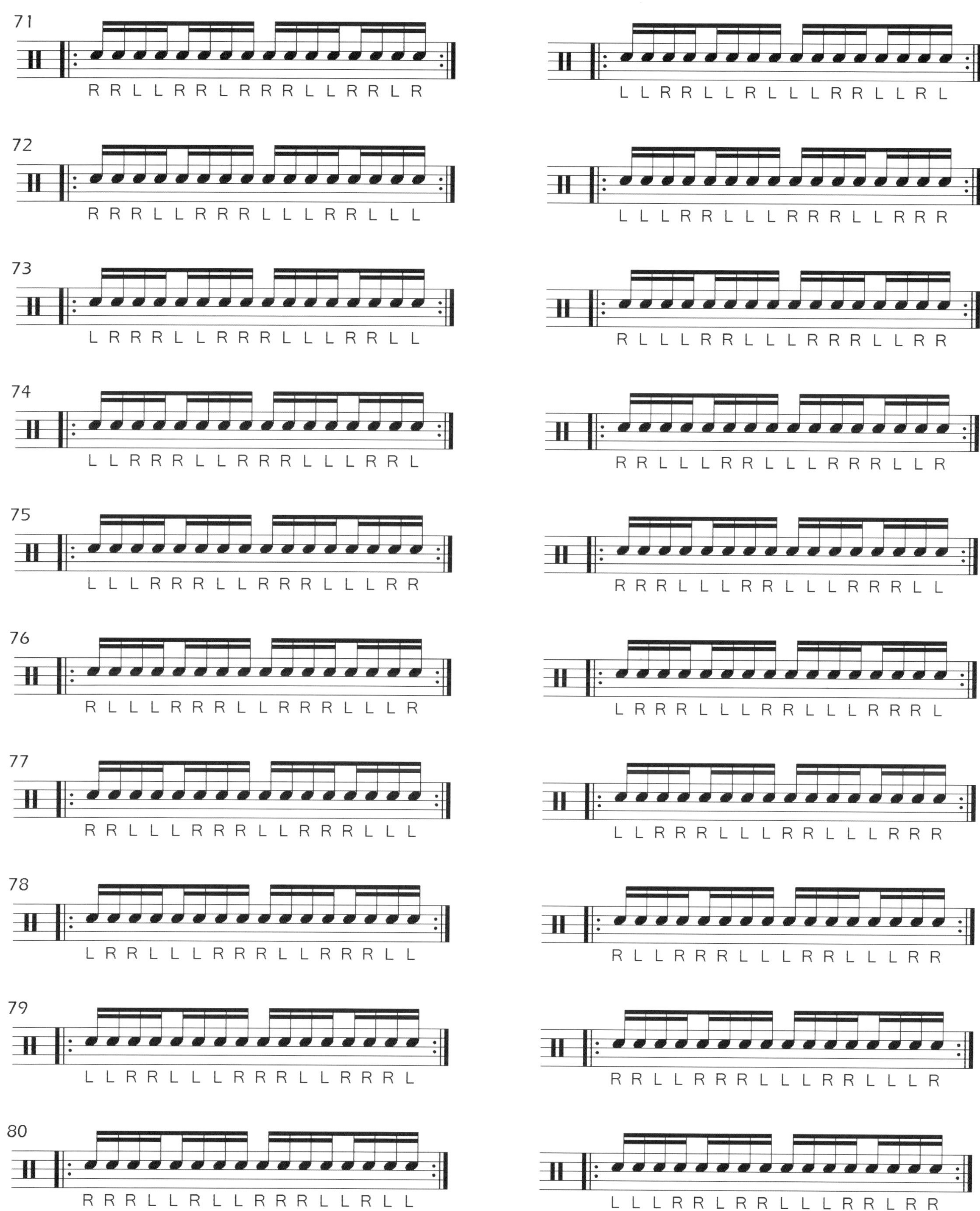

8-Note Combinations

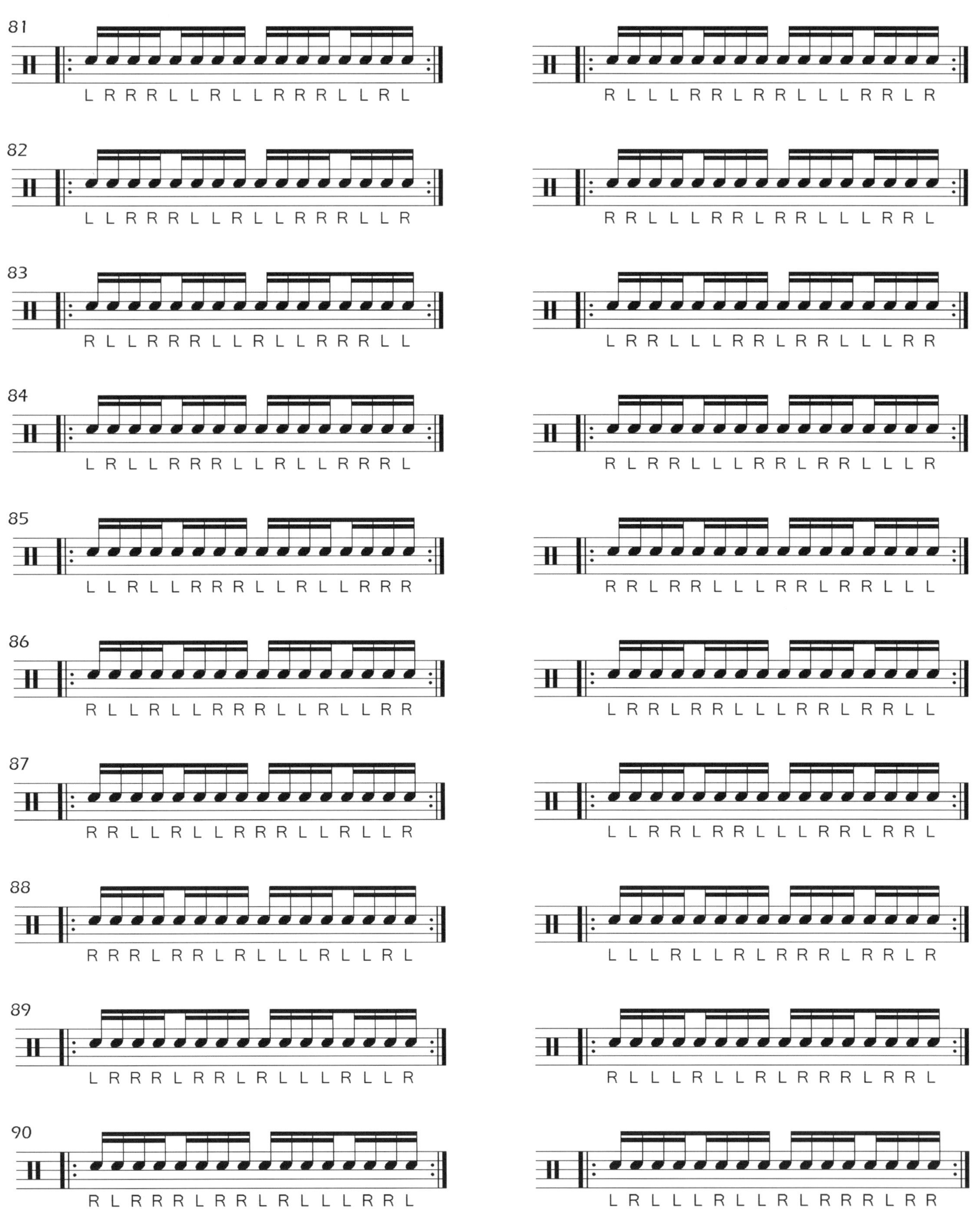

8-Note Combinations

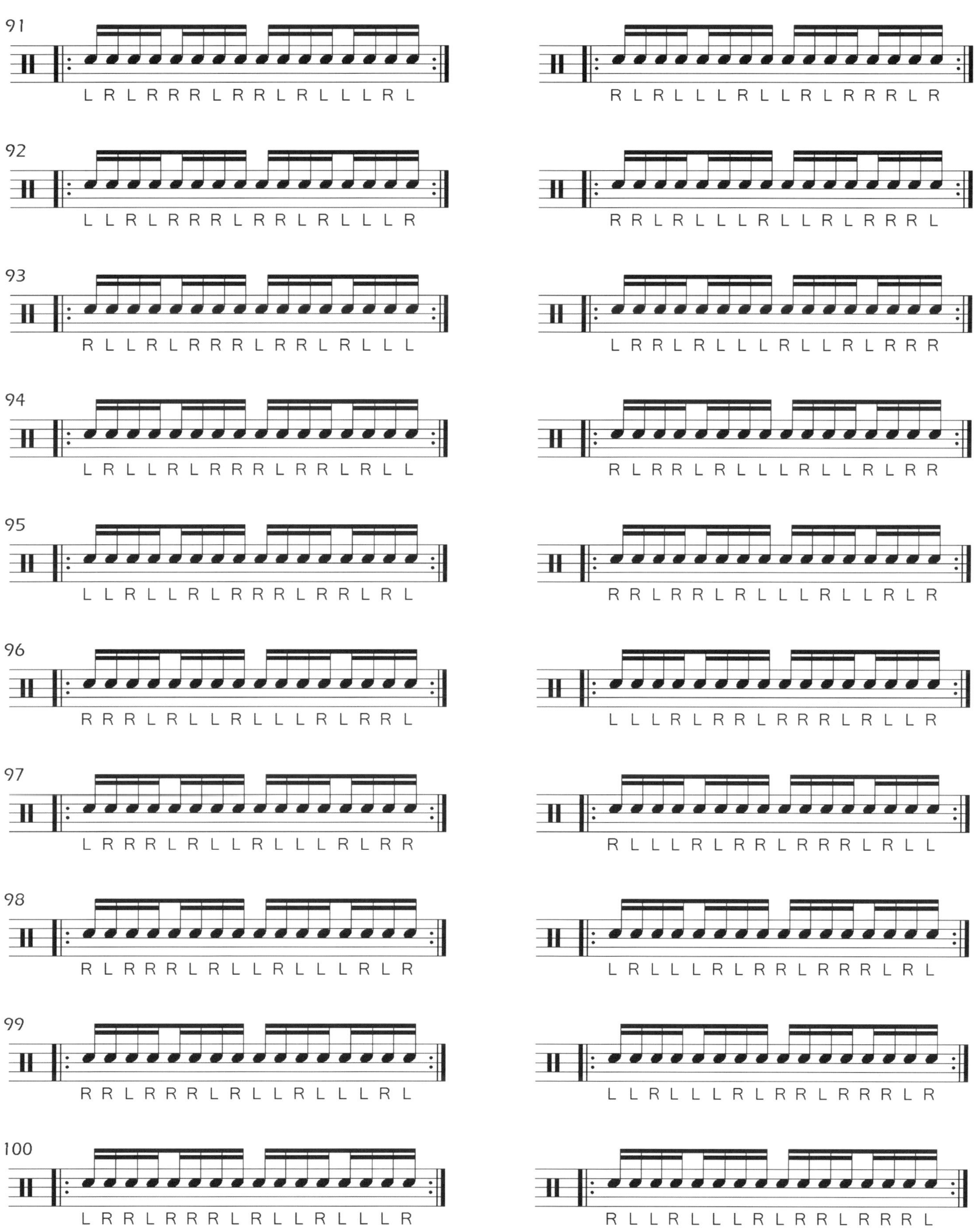

8-Note Combinations

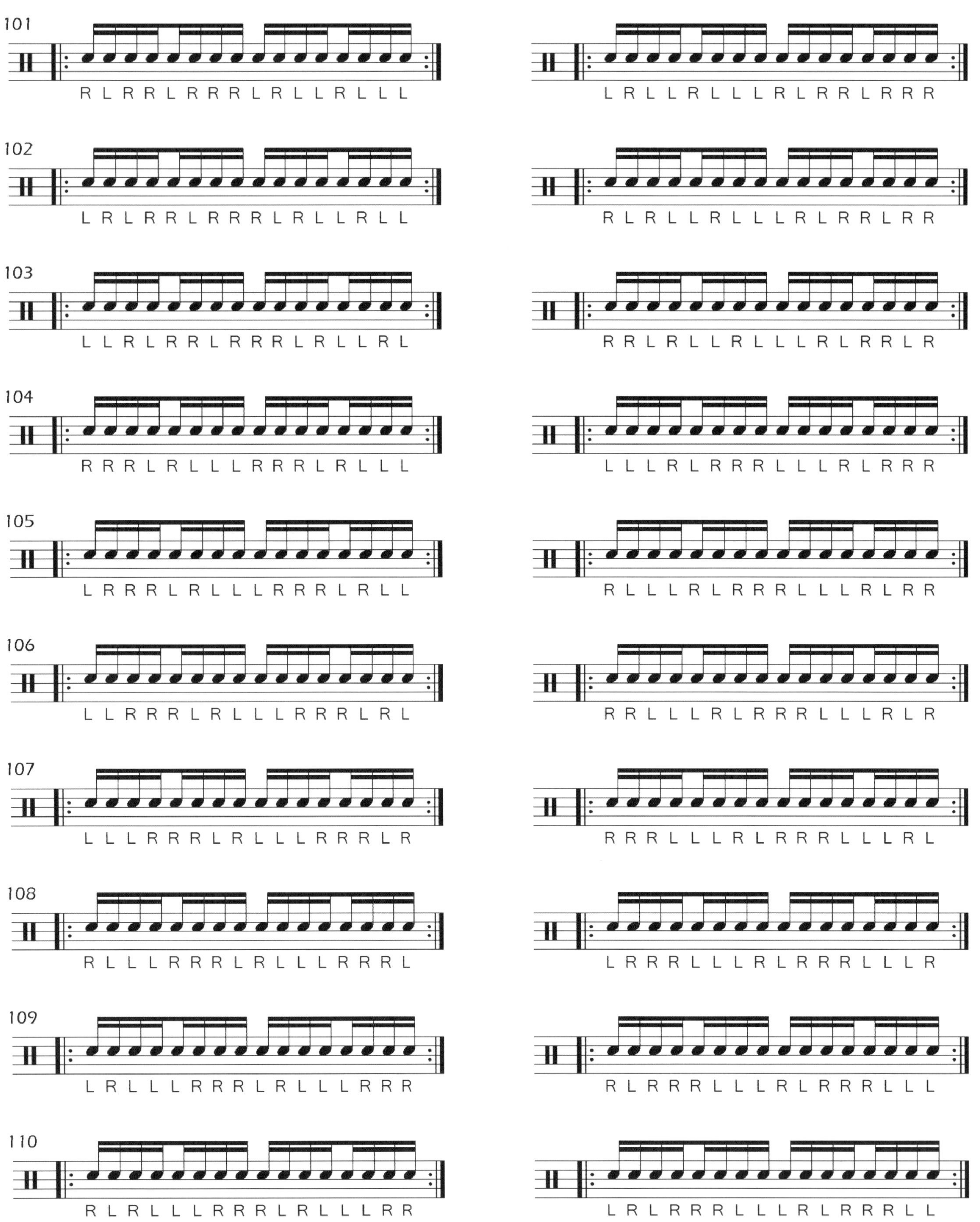

8-Note Combinations

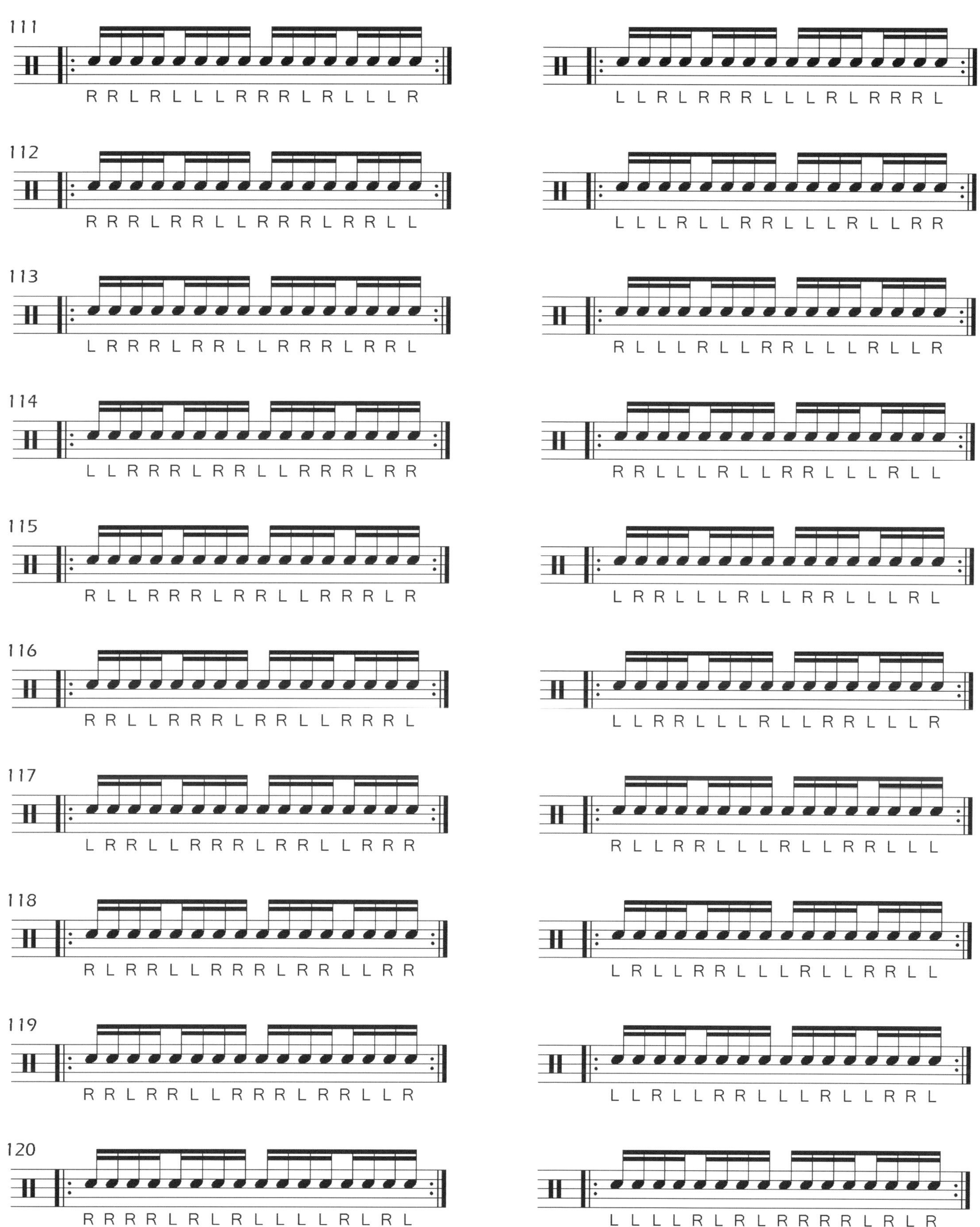

8-Note Combinations

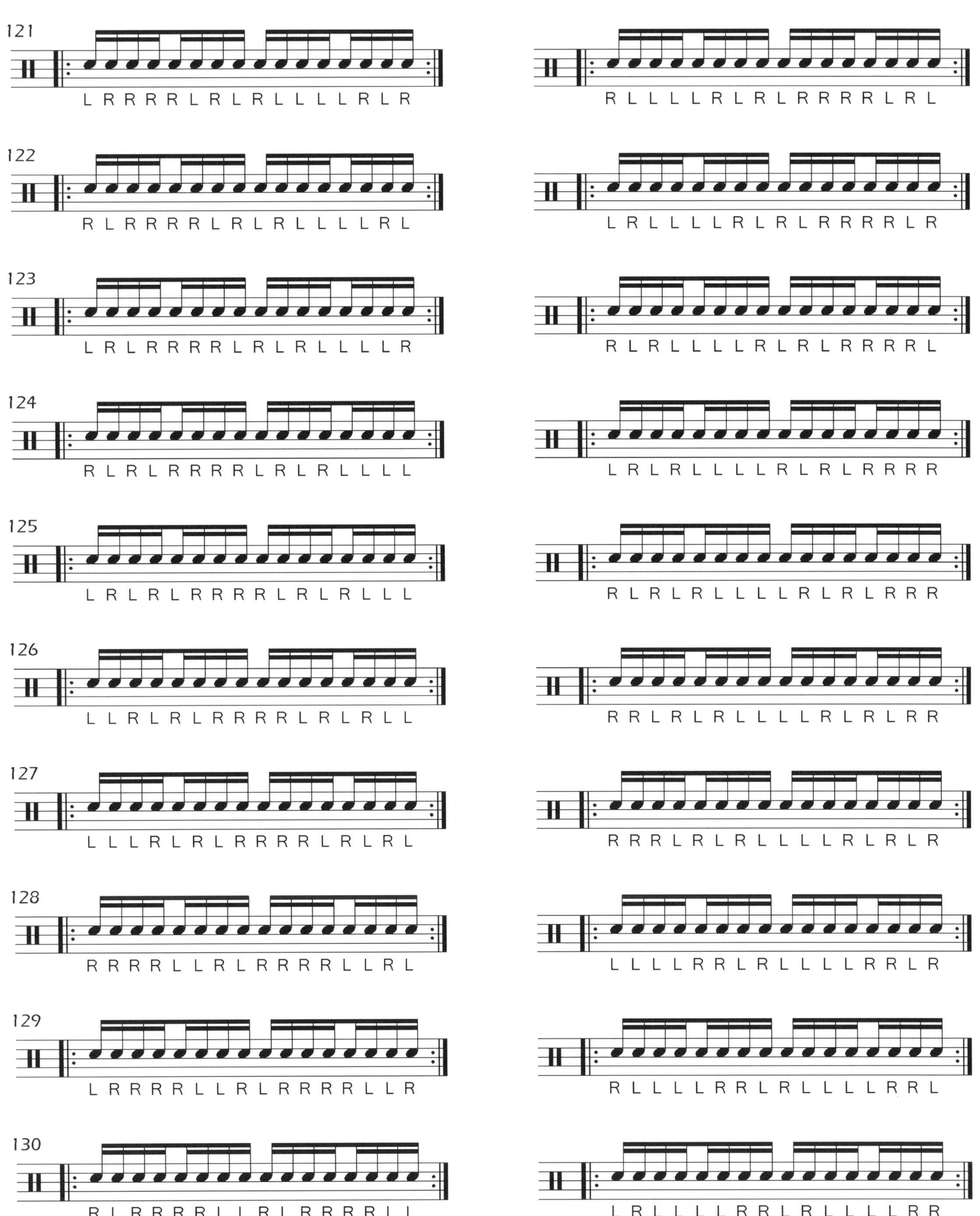

8-Note Combinations

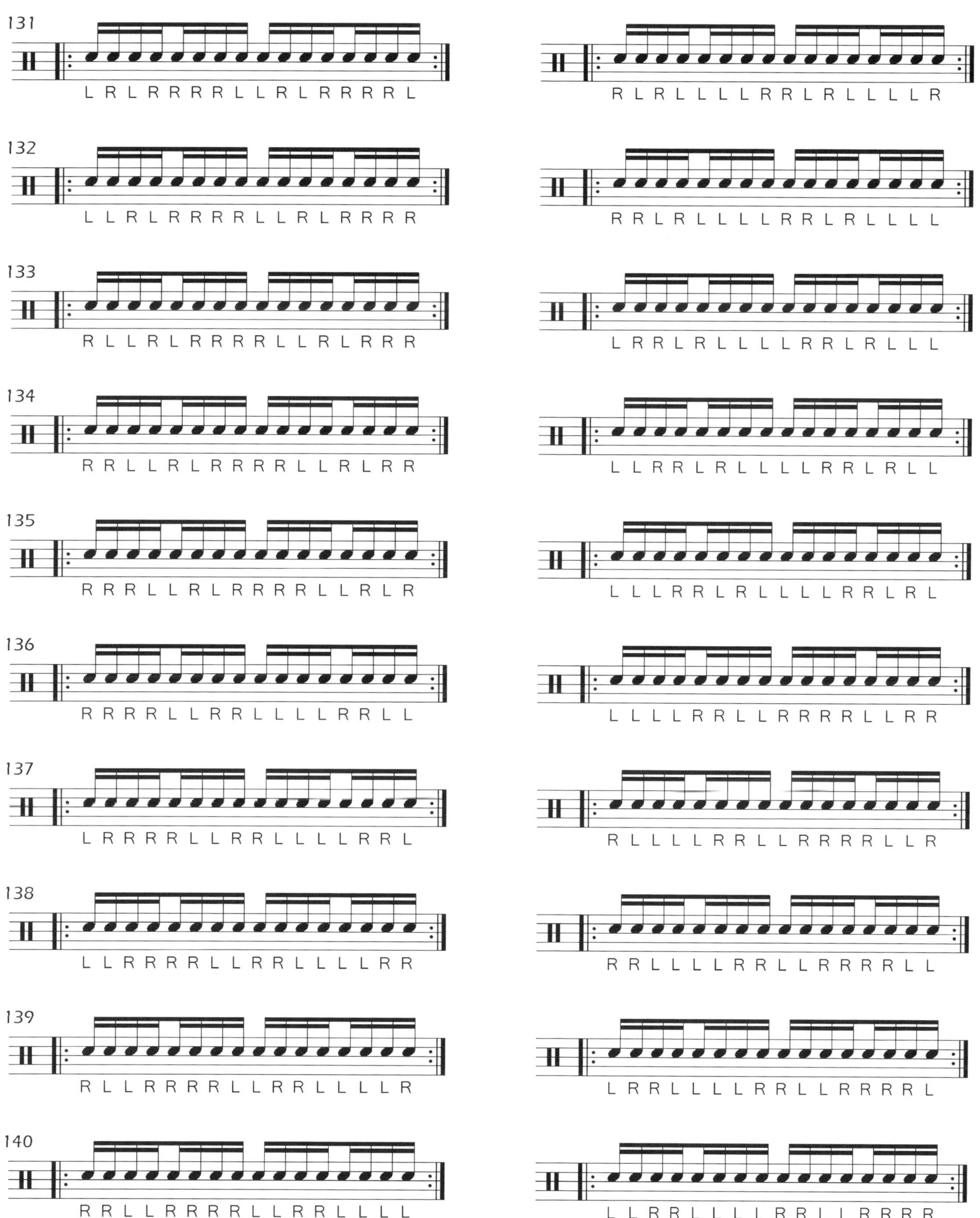

8-Note Combinations

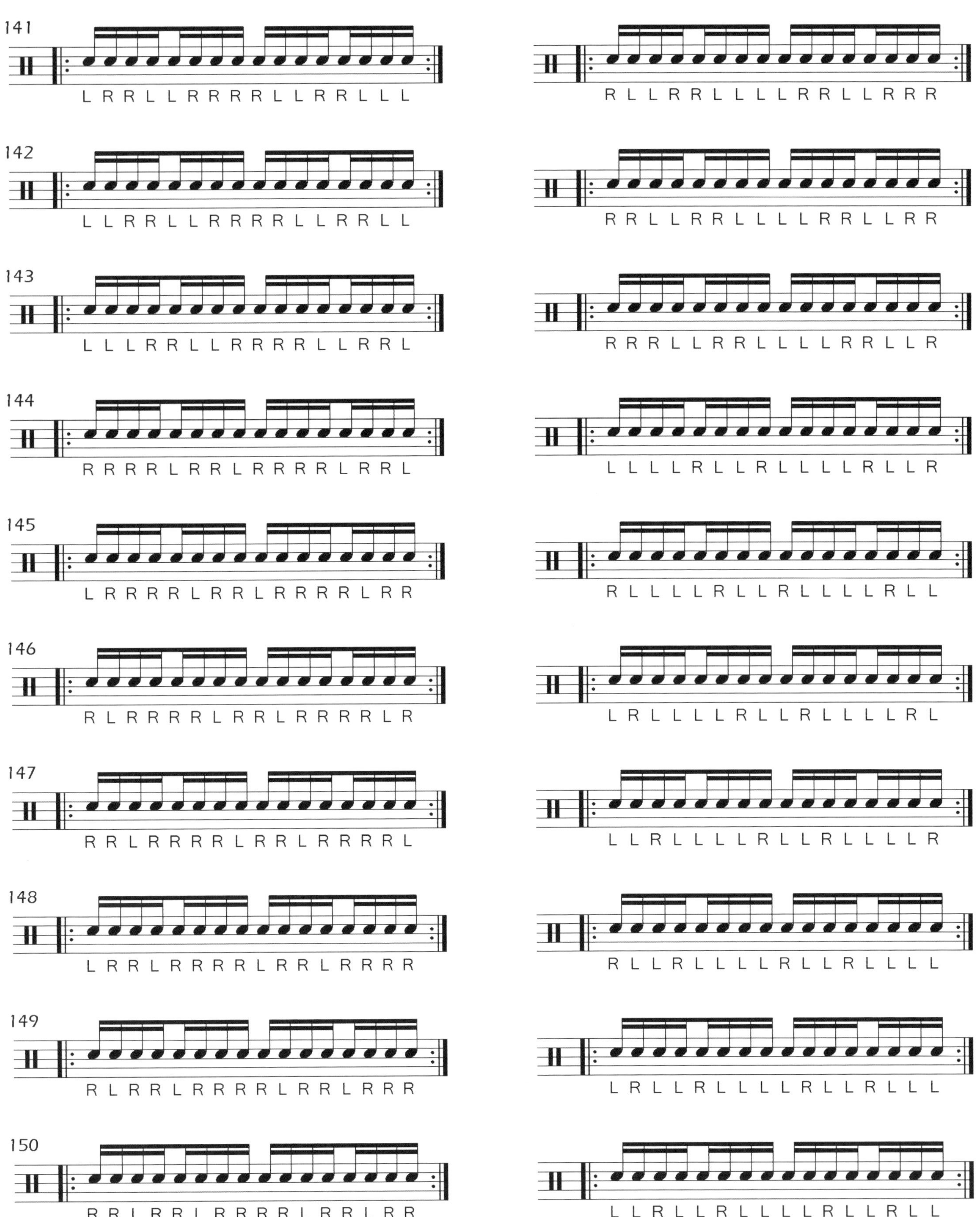

8-Note Combinations

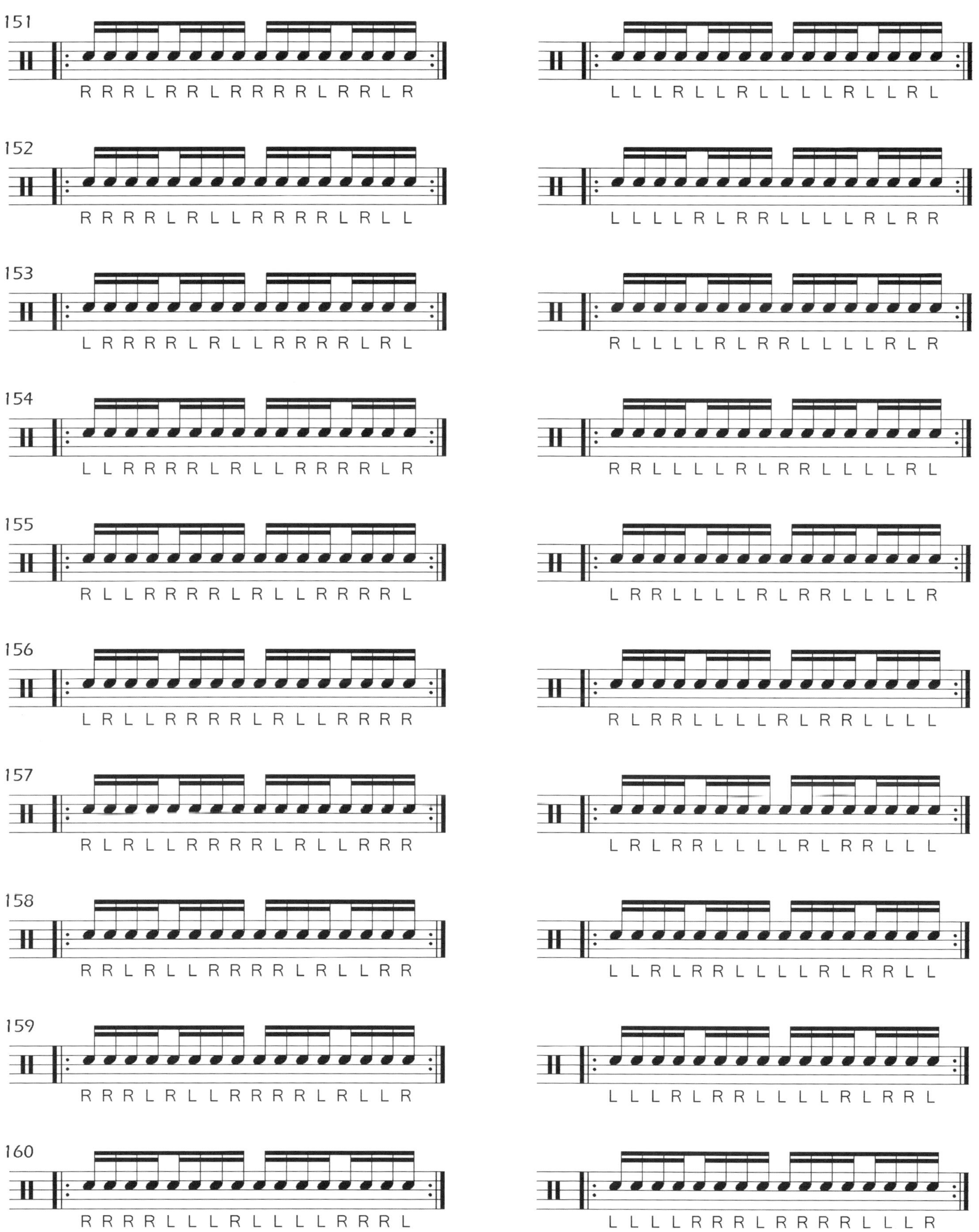

8-Note Combinations

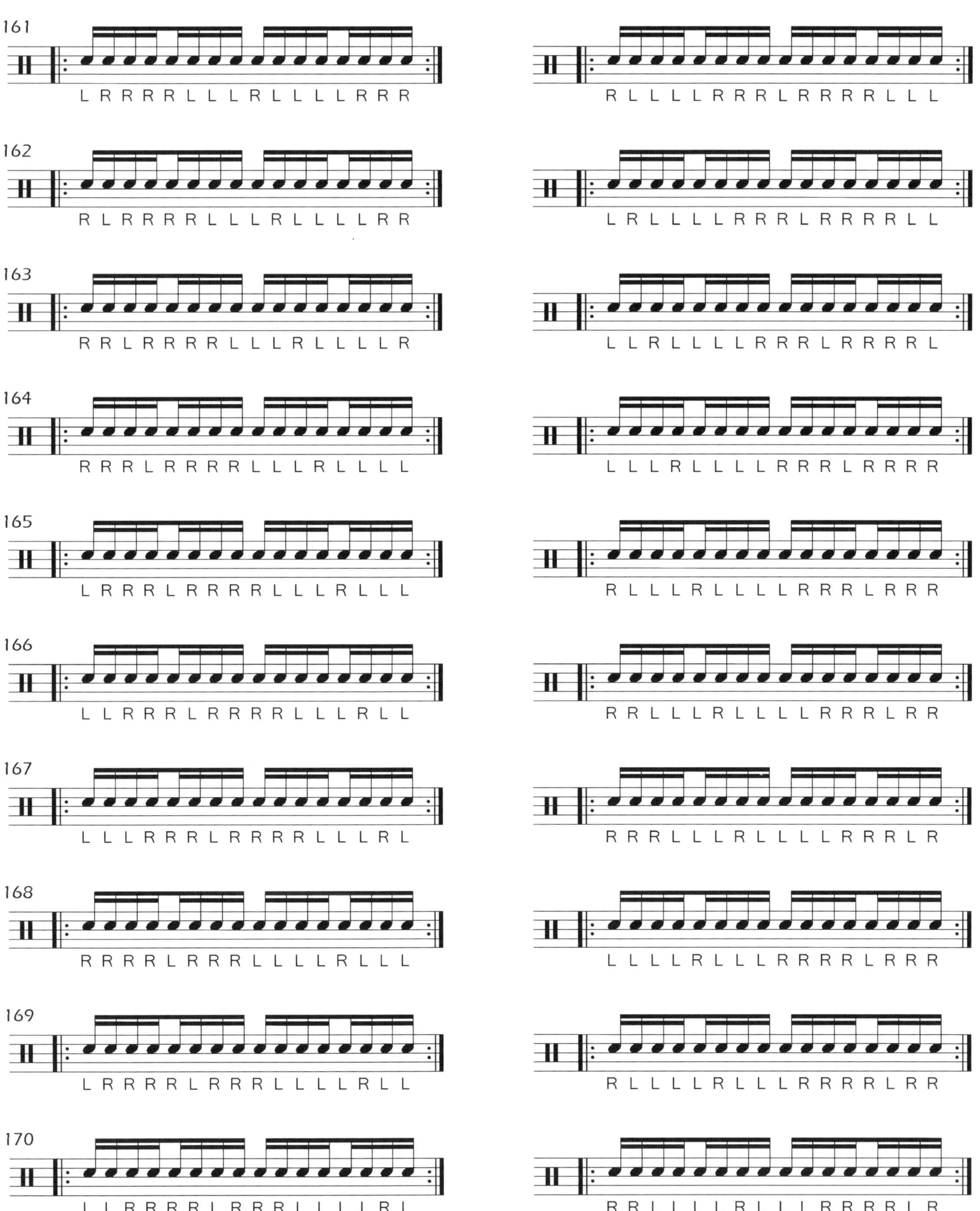

8-Note Combinations

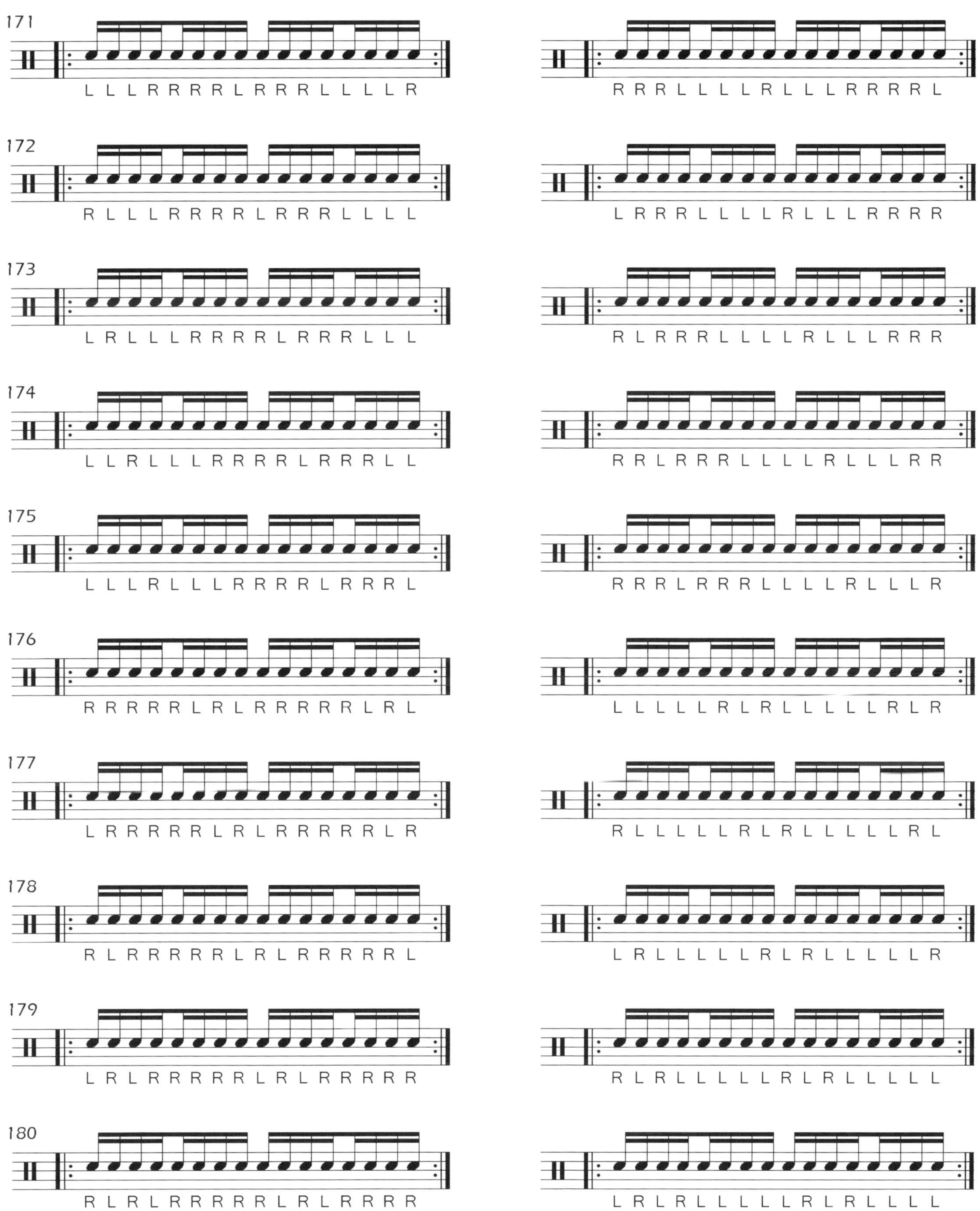

8-Note Combinations

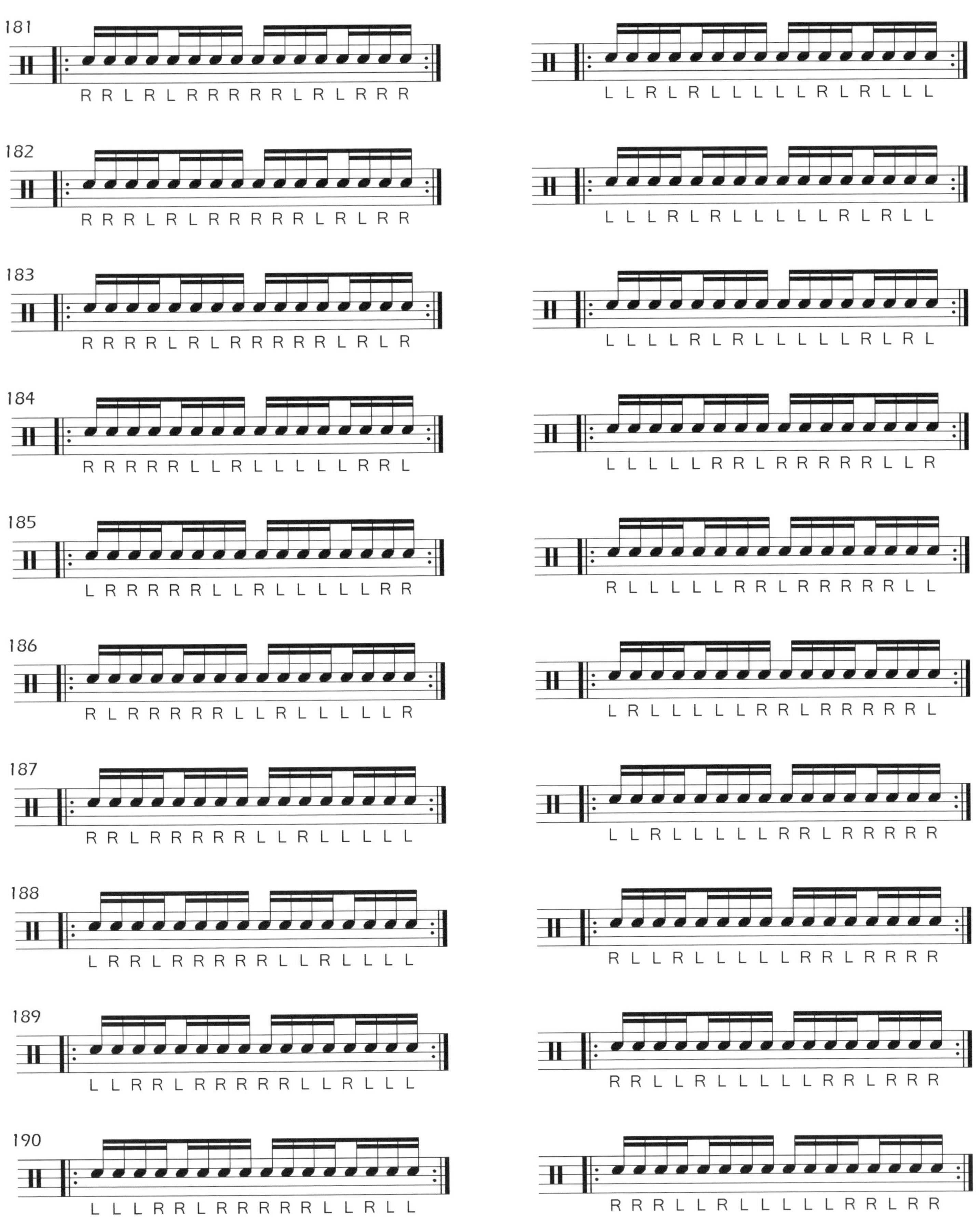

8-Note Combinations

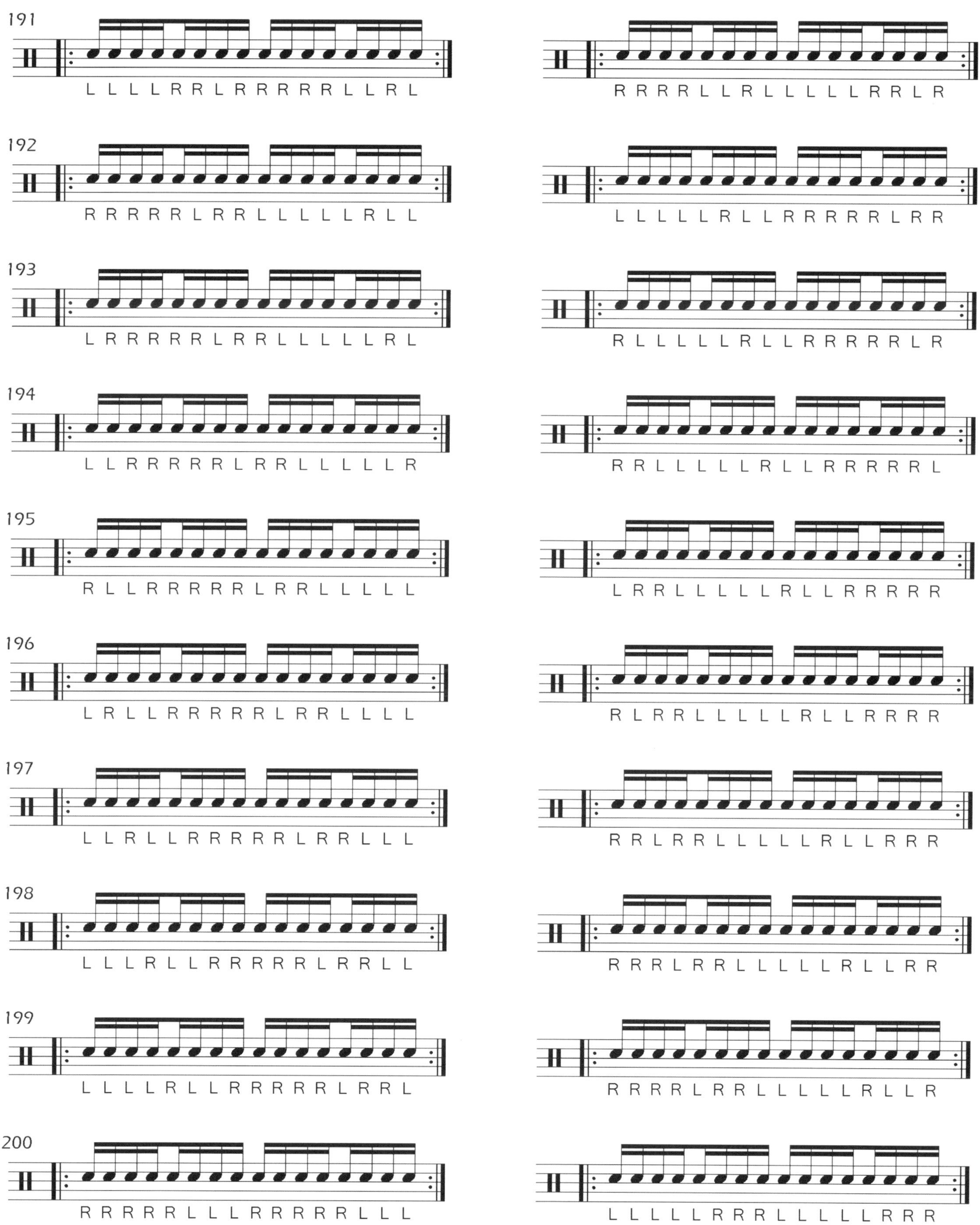

8-Note Combinations

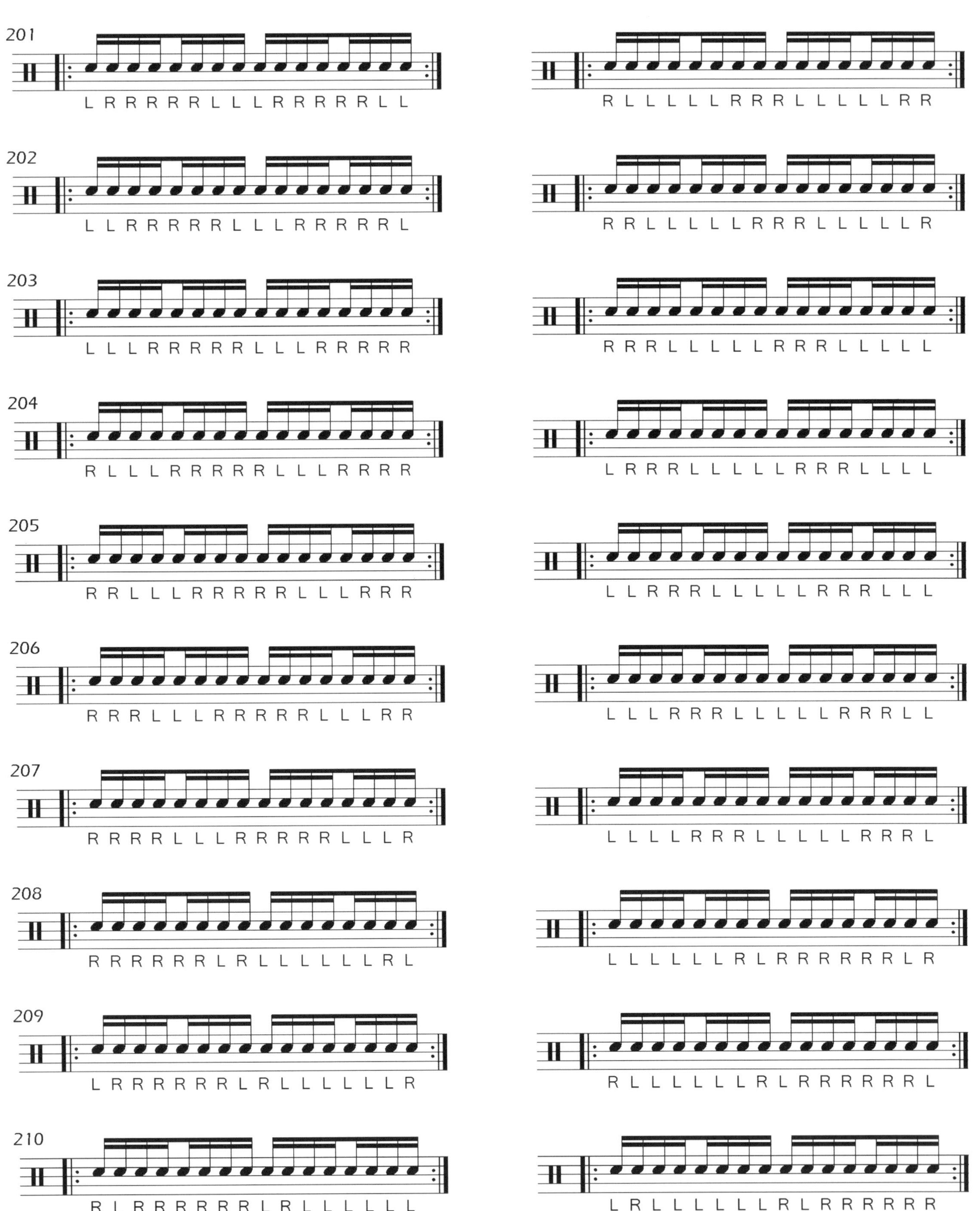

8-Note Combinations

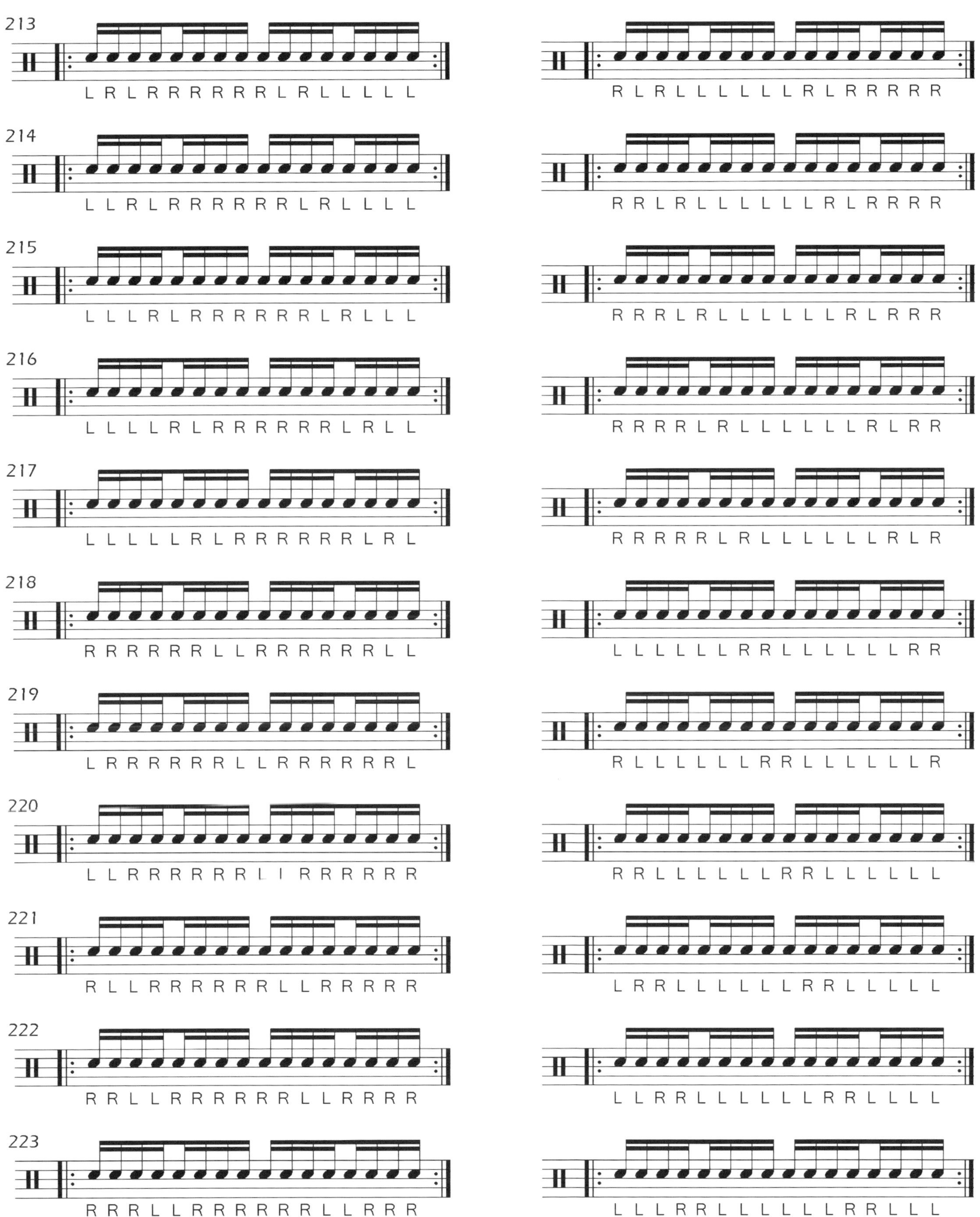

8-Note Combinations

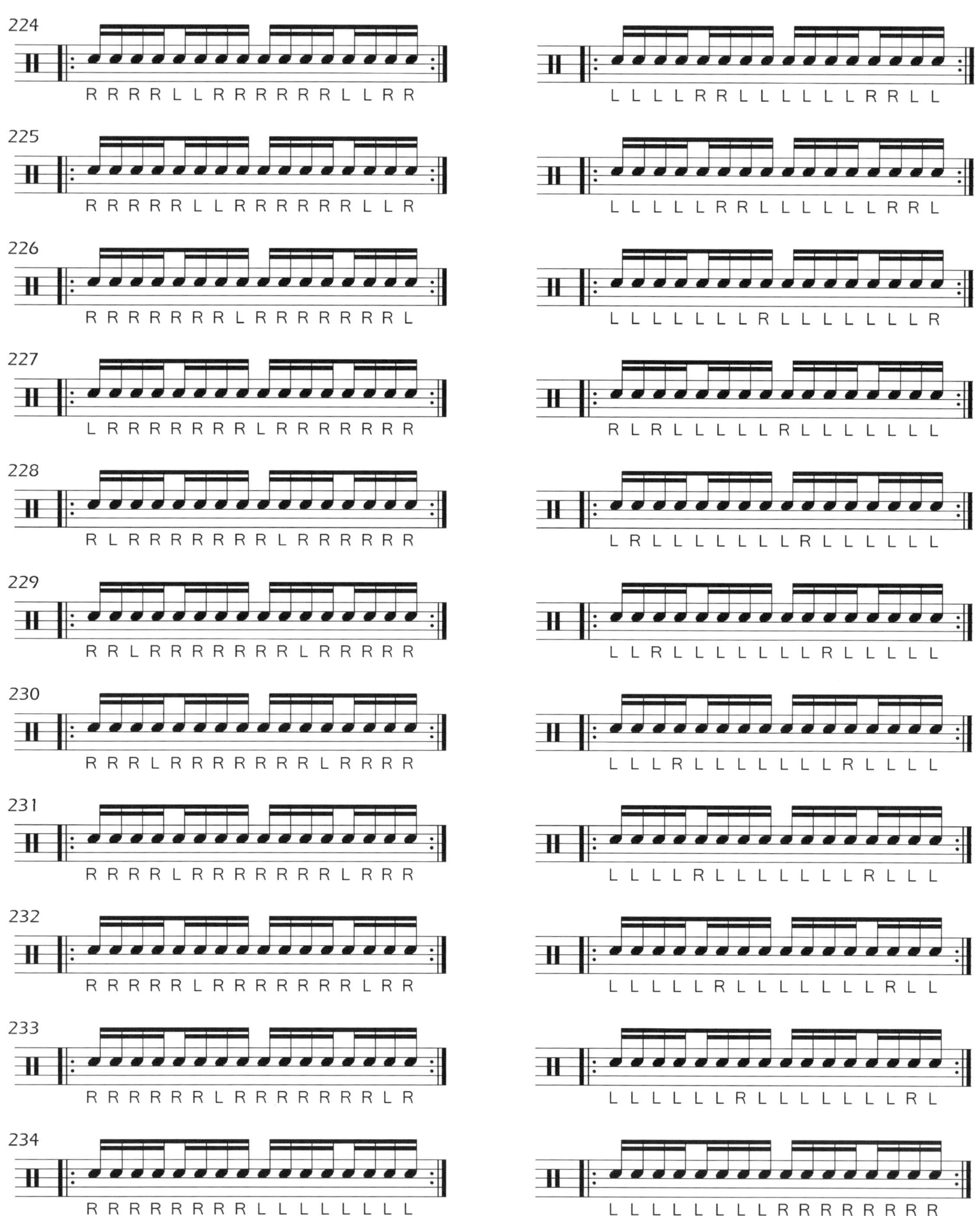

8-Note Combinations

- RHYTHM CHART -

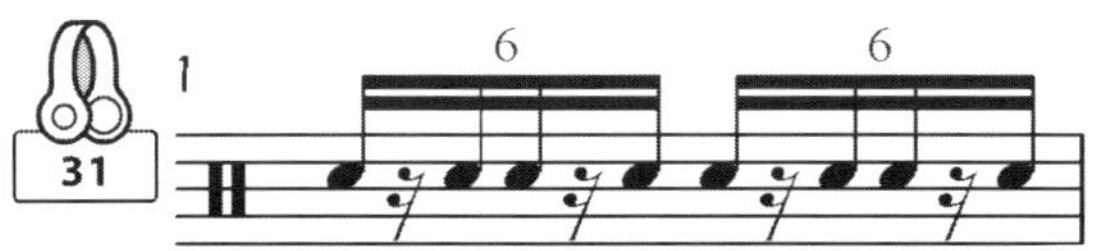

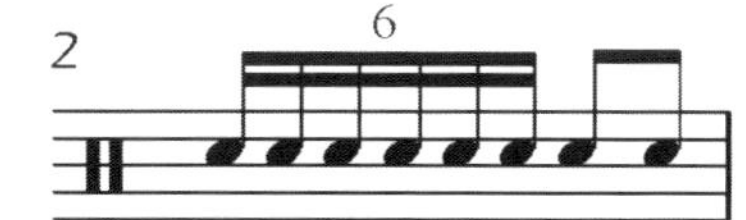

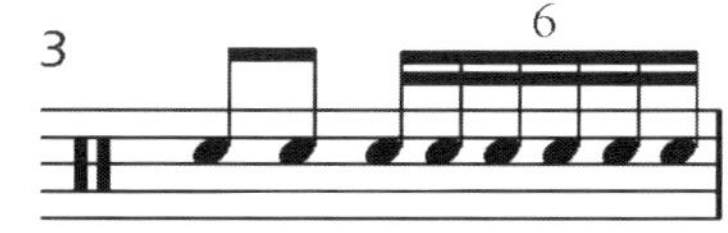

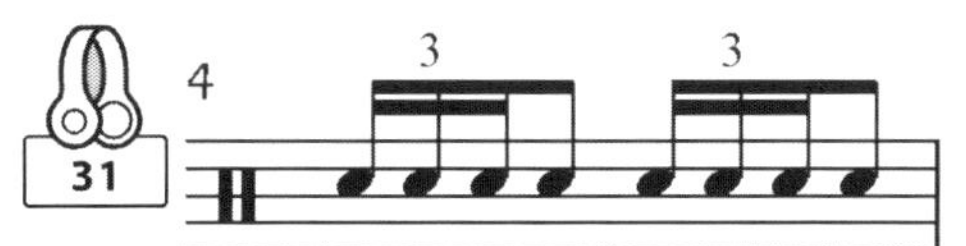

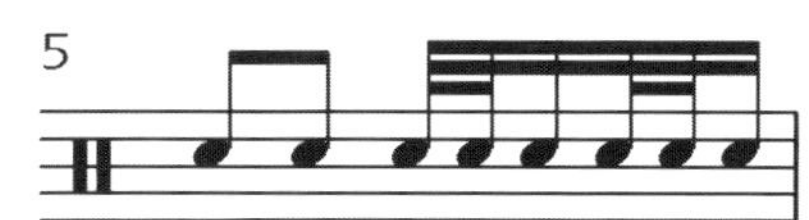

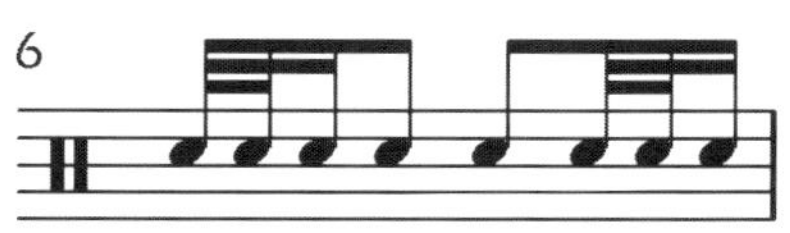

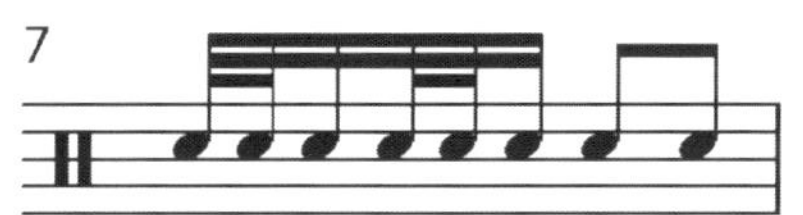

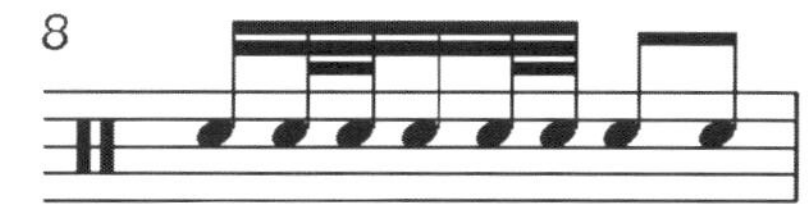

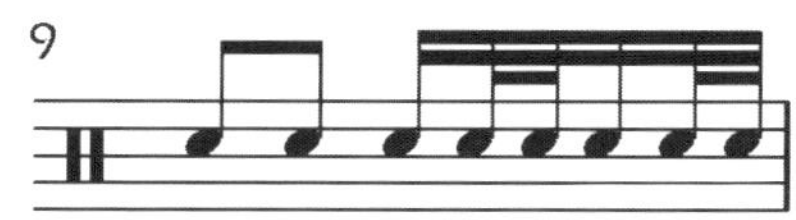

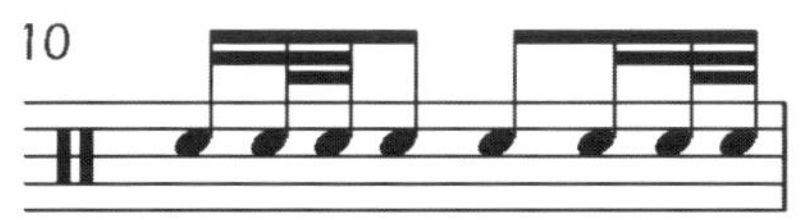

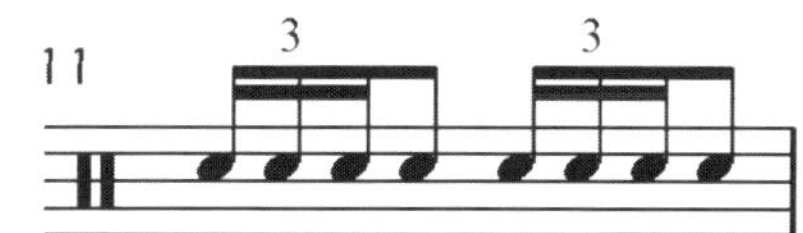

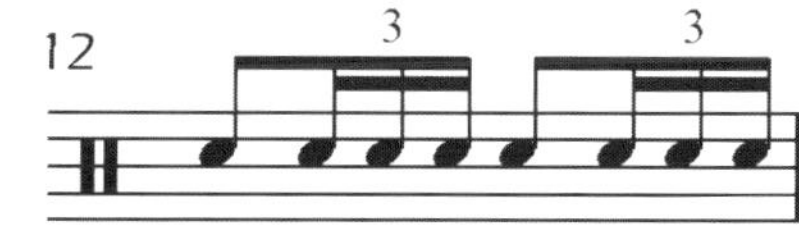

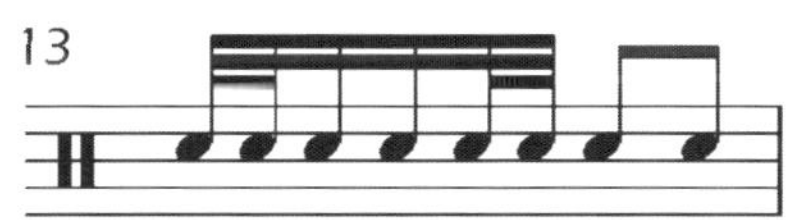

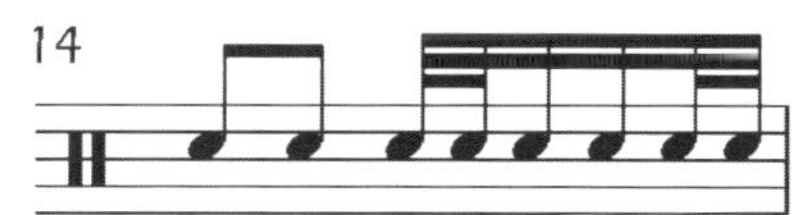

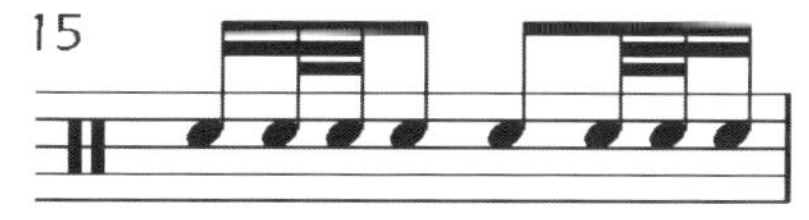

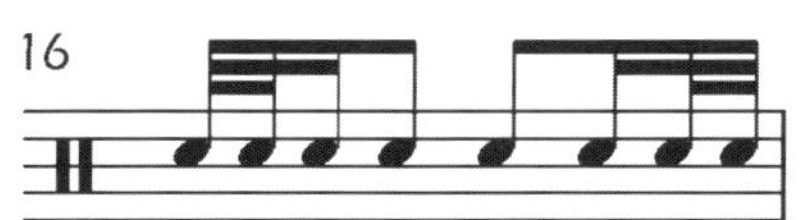

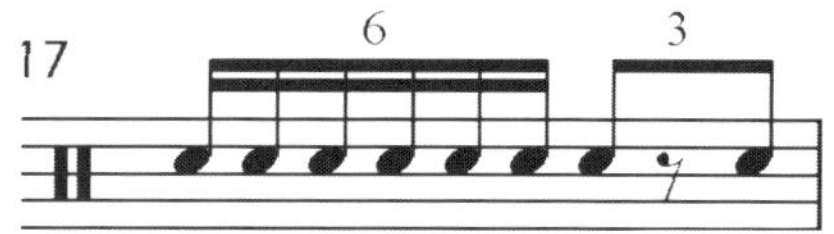

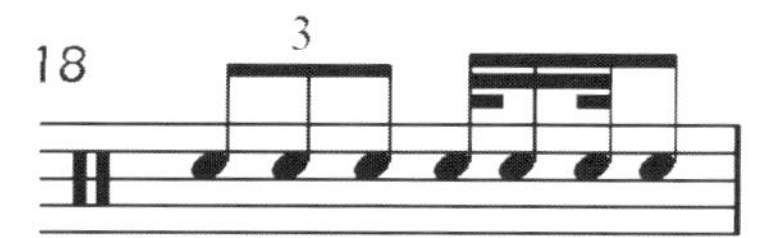

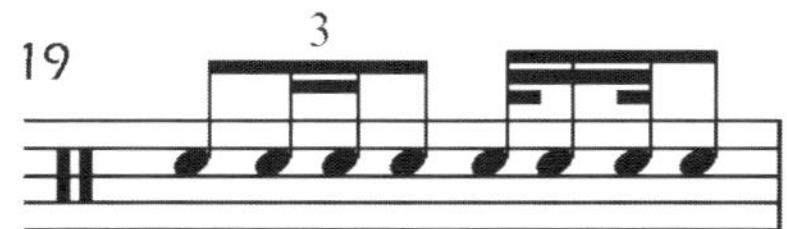

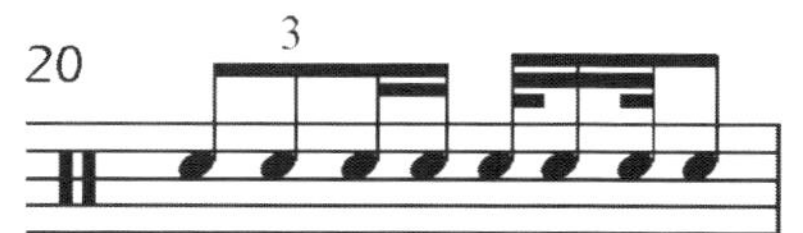

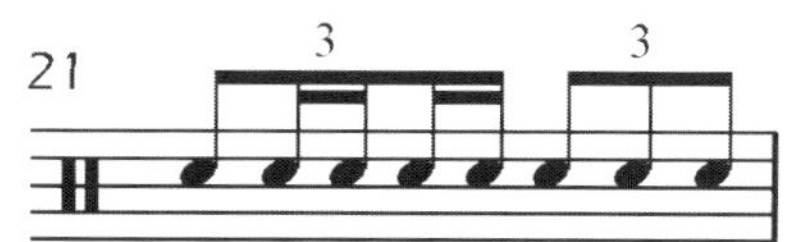

About the Author

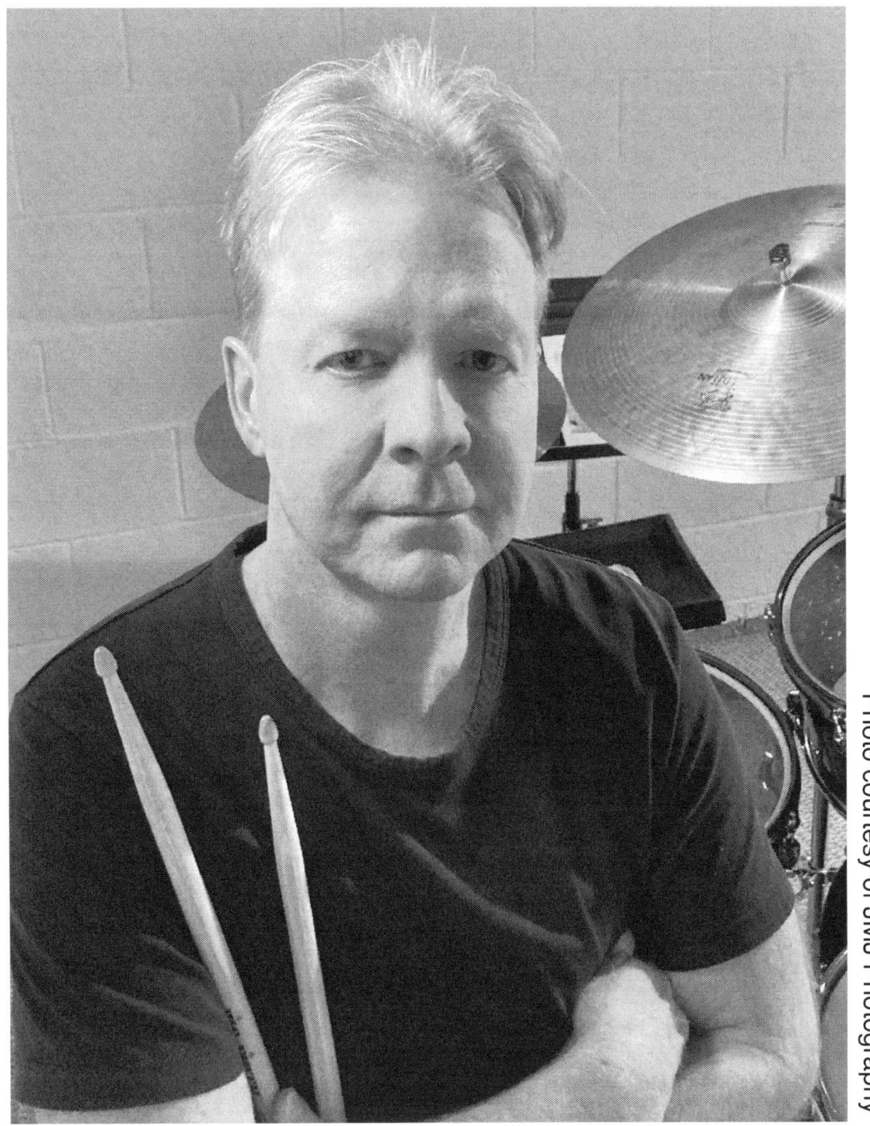

Photo courtesy of JMJ Photography

Kirby Jacobsen

Kirby Jacobsen—drummer, composer, author—has been playing drums professionally since the age of thirteen. He attended the University of Miami for Studio Music & Jazz and the William Paterson University for Jazz Performance.

Kirby has been a member of the Carmen Nappo youth Symphony, the Miami Beach Symphony and the Hanover Wind Symphony. He has performed extensively—both live and in the studio—with big bands and small combos, covering many musical styles including jazz, fusion, rock, Latin jazz and world music. He has performed live with notable musicians such as Ira Sullivan, Gary Campbell, Dave Liebman, Rafael Cruz and Jerry Jemmot. Kirby also leads the Blue Brush Trio which performs in the New York/New Jersey metro area.

Kirby is a published author of two books for solo snare drum: *Stick Twisters: A Dirty Dozen 'n One Solos for Snare Drum* and *Not Just Another Snare Solo Book: 20 Uncommon Solos for Snare Drum*. He has composed dozens of published pieces for percussion ensemble and snare drum as well. Kirby has contributed articles for *The Black Page Online Magazine*, DRUMGEEK.COM and *Rhythm! Scene* online publication of The Percussive Arts Society.

Other Mel Bay Drum Technique Books

Other Mel Bay Drum Technique Books

Hot Drum Grooves Made Easy/Large Print Edition (Morton)

Intro to Polyrhythms (Ari HoenigWeidenmueller)

Killer Fillers (Morton)

Killer Technique: Drumset (Green)

Learn to Burn: Drum Set (Perlson)

Learn to Burn: Drum Set Wall Chart (Prushko)

Mel Bay's Best Drumset Manuscript Book

Metric Modulations: Contracting & Expanding Time Within Form (Ari Hoenig/Weidenmueller)

Musical Drumset Solos for Recitals, Contests and Fun (Leyman)

Ostinatos for the Melodic Drumset (Leytham)

Paradiddles Redefined for Drum Set (Vega)

Rhythmic Aerobics (Ryan)

Rhythmic Aerobics, Vol. 2: Suffles, Swing, 6/8 & Odd-Times (Ryan)

Secrets of the Greats: Drumset Exercises for a Professional Sound (Silverman)

Steve Gadd Transcriptions (Gadd/Filipski)

Stick Tricks DVD (Ritter)

Studies in Drumset Independence Vol. 1 (Vinciguerra)

Studies in Drumset Independence Vol. 2 (Vinciguerra)

The Art of Transcribing: Drumset Book 1 (Schechner)

The Complete Blues/Rock Drummer (Ryan/Johnson)

The Drum Set Smart Book (Fidyk)

The Drum Set Styles Encyclopedia (Thomakos)

The Drummer's Workbook (D. Gottlieb/M. Green)

The Gears for Grooving on Drumset (Brennenstuhl)

The Rhythm Encyclopedia (Woods)

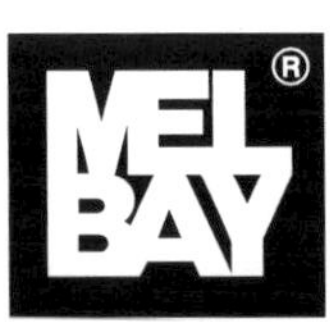

WWW.MELBAY.COM